EVANGELISM BY FIRE

The Revd Reinhard Bonnke is founder-leader of Christ for all Nations (CfaN), an evangelistic missionary society begun in 1974 as a servant to the church, with main offices in Frankfurt in Germany, and organising offices in East and West Africa, England and the USA.

The collaborating writer of this book is the Revd George Canty, a church pioneer and world travelled journalist, who has written several books and has been an evangelist since 1954.

Evangelism by Fire

An Initiative for Revival

REINHARD BONNKE

with George Canty

KINGSWAY PUBLICATIONS
EASTBOURNE

First published 1989
Reprinted 1989
Reprinted 1990

Biblical quotations are from the
Authorised Version, Crown copyright, unless otherwise marked.

Front cover photo: The Image Bank

British Library Cataloguing in Publication Data

Bonnke, Reinhard
 Evangelism by fire.
 1. Christian church. Evangelism
 I. Title
 269'.2

 ISBN 0-86065-809-0

Printed in Great Britain for
KINGSWAY PUBLICATIONS LTD
1 St Anne's Road, Eastbourne, E Sussex BN21 3UN by
Richard Clay Ltd, Bungay, Suffolk.
Typeset by Nuprint Ltd, Harpenden, Herts AL5 4SE.

To the inspiring memory of
my unforgettable brothers, friends and
CfaN team workers,

HORST KOSANKE and MILTON KASSELMAN

who laid down their lives for the gospel of Jesus Christ
in Africa,
ascending to glory in chariots of fire,
to receive their crown of life from the Lord.

Contents

How Big Is Hell?

When I was a young missionary in Africa, I worked on what was considered to be the proper methods of missions. My heart, nevertheless, longed to see the vast multitudes of precious African people rejoicing in Christ. The 'tried and proved' methods of traditional missionary endeavour, the way I was doing it, had only proved that a minute percentage of those around ever responded.

God took hammer and chisel and began working on me. Things didn't shape up overnight. I learned lessons one by one. New dimensions of the Holy Spirit opened, each one an astonishment to me. Signs and wonders began to occur. There is no formula for instant success 'on the cheap'.

What God led me to see over the years, through many an experience and always through His word, I want to share in this book. I do so to inspire evangelism. I have laid out here the principles which are recognisable in any truly Holy Spirit-led ministry. The Lord needs servants, old or new. I hope that my book will throw further light on how God operates.

During the writing of this book, we have seen as many

as 150,000 people claiming salvation in a single meeting, and two million in a single year. Our crowds are greater than ever. Multitudes have been healed and filled with the Holy Spirit. I treasure in my heart what I believe is God's assurance that, one day, we shall gather in a harvest of one million souls in a single meeting.

We have seen whole countries shaken by the power of the gospel of Jesus Christ. If this can be the result of things God has shown me, my hope is that God will show others, also. May they have that heart revelation of the matchless glory of His power, a power beyond anything I have ever seen (or anyone else has ever seen, for that matter). The potentials of Pentecost have never yet been fully utilised, and there is much more to come.

Two thoughts long have thundered in my soul. First, the vision God gave me of a blood-washed Africa. Second, the principle of plundering hell to populate heaven. To me, these are not mere notions of far-fetched ideals, but words from God which He will fulfil. God will not give the whole world to any one man or woman. He wants to raise up an *army* of anointed people.

God is the Creator of evangelists, ordinary flesh-and-blood folk. Angels probably could have done a far more efficient job, but in the infinite wisdom of the Lord, He had no such plan. If that is so, we humans are privileged. There should be no reluctance on our part to do this work.

It is striking to consider, that the angel who appeared to Cornelius in Acts 10 was not allowed to mention the name of Jesus, or to speak about salvation to the man. All the angel could say was, 'Now send men to Joppa and call for one Simon, whose surname is Peter....' This mighty seraph from deep heaven had to bow to Peter's higher privilege. We only can accept, with wonder and humility, the fact that it pleases God to call and to send people like you and me.

It has always been the same. God used four evangelists—Matthew, Mark, Luke and John—to write down the story of the gospel of Jesus Christ. Such a pattern is linked, in my mind, to the four men in Old Testament times who carried the Ark of the Covenant. Carriers of the gospel change from generation to generation, but the gospel remains the same. Now we are here, and today it is our turn. God has called you and me. The gospel needs to be taken to the ends of the earth. This is the Great Commission of the Lord to us, and the King's business requires haste.

These chapters are written because I do not believe that God's plans allow hell to be bigger than heaven. Although Scripture speaks about 'many' who are on their way to eternal destruction (Mt 7:13), they must be intercepted by men and women preaching the original gospel. Provision has been made to bring 'many sons into glory' (Heb 2:10) and Revelation 7:9 speaks of a successful conclusion. 'Disciple all nations...' Jesus instructed. There are no emergency arrangements in case the gospel fails. It won't! More people are being saved, healed and baptised into the Holy Spirit today than ever before in man's history. The tempo must increase, however. Jesus is coming soon.

We are not called with the outcome of an uncertain war hanging in the balance. We are called to share the victory and the spoils. God's invincible secret is the cross of Christ, which frightens every demon in hell. Heaven will be an eternal and dominating monument to the victory of the gospel. These pages are a welcome to join a conquering army, not a plea to support a hopeless and desperate resistance against overwhelming odds. Our Captain never lost a battle, and He never will.

For this purpose, God has laid down the basic means for the salvation of souls. Human schemes have not been the answer, and if we follow them we will see the present generation die in their sins. The mighty commission of Christ to His church is a call-up to the war against unbelief, using the sword of the gospel as our weapon.

I am not concerned with means and methods in this book, but with spiritual principles. I have, in fact, tried to encourage individual enterprise and initiative. God will give us resourcefulness. There are as many methods as He directs.

We need more imaginative approaches rather than doing things a certain way just because that's the way they always have been done. Methods which have made little impact in the past are not likely to produce an impact now. Plodding along 'mechanically' might be called faithfulness, but our primary concern in evangelism is effectiveness, not this type of faithfulness.

I am concerned, because there surely must be limiting factors hindering the gospel. What these may be is not the direct purpose of this book. These limiting factors possibly are the accepted methods of evangelism, which are still unchanged. They could even be doctrines and sentiments which tell us to 'leave it all to God'. Some insist God's way is revival, but they fail to carry out the Great Commission in the meanwhile. Some think that if people are to be saved, they will be saved anyway. Suppose such theories are wrong? After all, they surely are! What an awful risk, to rest the eternal destiny of souls upon a controversial interpretation of a scripture or the turn of a Greek verb. We dare not neglect the task of evangelism. Let us be sure.

I think that when you read these pages, you perhaps will find that their temperature is high. This book is hot— its flames will catch. Its message is not one-sided, but it does come from a singleness of heart. I hammer away at the Great Commission, but it cannot be overemphasised. I cry to God day and night for greater effectiveness in winning our generation for Him. *Evangelism by fire* is the only feasible solution.

I constantly scan the horizons for other anointed men and women who may take up this challenge of the word of God for Holy Ghost evangelism. I believe the best is yet to be. The whole world will resound with the praises of our God and Saviour. In all nations and in every tongue, confession will be made that Jesus Christ is Lord, to the glory of God the Father.

PART ONE

The Need

I

When Arson Is Not a Crime

Somebody said that God sets driftwood on fire. Hallelujah! Dry old sticks can burn for God, just like Moses' bush did!

I don't pray, 'Let me burn out for thee, dear Lord.' I don't want to be an ash heap. The amazing feature of the bush was that it didn't burn out. Too many of the Lord's servants are burning out. The cause of that is some other kind of fire. I say instead, 'Let me *burn on* for thee, dear Lord.' The altar flame should never go out.

Without fire, there is no gospel. The New Testament begins with fire. The first thing said about Christ by His first witness concerned fire. John the Baptist, himself a 'burning and shining light', declared: 'He shall baptize you with the Holy Ghost, and with fire: Whose fan is in his hand, and he will throughly purge his floor, and gather his wheat into the garner; but he will burn up the chaff with unquenchable fire' (Mt 3:11–12).

John the baptiser introduced Jesus the Baptiser, the Baptiser with a vast difference. John used water, a physical element, but Christ was to use a spiritual element, the

Holy Spirit. Water and fire—what a contrast! Not that John the Baptist had a watery religion—there is plenty of that around, often combined with ice! John the Baptist stood in the cold waters of Jordan, baptising, but Jesus the Baptiser stood in a river of liquid fire.

The notable work of John was baptism. He announced the notable work of Jesus as baptism also. Baptism is the Lord's present great work. Jesus the Baptiser—in the Holy Spirit. If you are a born-again believer, this is Christ's major experience for you.

Incendiarists

The gospel is a firelighter. The Holy Spirit is not given just to help you preach eloquent sermons. He is to put a flame into human hearts. Unless Christ sets you alight, you can bring no fire to earth. 'Without me, ye can do nothing,' said the Lord (Jn 15:5). Jesus instructed the disciples not to do anything until they were to 'receive power from on high'. When that power came, the Spirit revealed himself as tongues of flame sitting upon each one of them.

Jesus previously had sent the disciples out in pairs (Lk 10:1). It reminds me of Samson sending foxes out two by two, as the animals carried torches for an arson raid on the enemy's corn shocks and vineyards (Judg 15). The disciples also were sent out two by two, carriers of the divine torch, incendiaries for God, scorching the Devil's territories with the fire gospel. They were new Elijahs bringing fire from heaven.

Until the fire falls, evangelism and church activities can be very routine and unexciting. Pulpit essays, homilies, moralising or preaching about how you think the economy of the country should be run—all that is glacial work. No divine spark brings combustion to ice. No one goes home ignited. In contrast, the two who listened to Jesus on the Emmaus road went home with warmed hearts. I am sure He didn't talk politics to them, nor offer suggestions and advice. That wouldn't make their hearts burn. Jesus came 'to scatter fire on earth'.

The mission of Jesus is not a holiday picnic—Satan is determined it will not be. He is a destroyer. The Lord sends out His servants with a warning of physical dangers. 'Fear not them which kill the body, but are not able to kill the soul; but rather fear him which is able to destroy both soul and body in hell.' What is mere physical hurt, compared to a life ablaze with the joy and zest of Jesus? What is bodily danger compared to the crown of life, or to the wonderful work He gives us to do? 'Heal the sick, cleanse the lepers, raise the dead, cast out devils; freely ye have received, freely give' (Mt 10:28, 8).

The sign of the Son of Man

Fire is the ensign of the gospel, the sign of the Son of Man. Only Jesus baptises in fire. When we see such baptisms, that is the evidence that He, and nobody else, is at work. It is the identifying hallmark of His activity and of the true Christian faith at large. Put your hand on such activities, and you will feel the heat. The prophet Elijah made the same point—'The God that answereth by fire, let him be God' (1 Kings 18:24). Only one God does that. Elijah was sure that Baal was incapable of it.

What does your spiritual thermometer read? Does it even register? Are you chilled? Are there cold altars in the church? Worship without warmth? Doctrines heated only by friction?

There are theologies and teachings as heavy and as inflammable as lead. There are religious books that only provide heat if put on a bonfire. Such faith-chilling items have nothing to do with the Christ of Pentecost. Whatever He touches, catches light. Jesus melts the ice. Some church efforts to whip up a little enthusiasm are, spiritually, like rubbing two sticks together.

Dummy ammunition

The fire of God is special—unique. Only the fire of God
was allowed on the altar of Moses, not fire produced by
any human means. Nadab and Abihu made fire themselves and lit their incense with it. It was labelled 'strange
fire'. Divine fire gushed from the tabernacle, swallowing
up the false fire and bringing about the deaths of the rebel
priests (Num 26:61).

Today, we have strange fire being offered. Strange gospels which are not gospels at all, theologies of unbelief.
The thoughts of men and their philosophies, criticisms
and theories. They bear no trace of the glory-heat from
heaven. Nothing in them produces any combustion except
controversy.

What lies behind all this is something which my friend
Paul C Schoch pointed out to me. He quoted Matthew
16:23, where Jesus addressed Satan when speaking to the
apostle Peter: 'Get thee behind me, Satan: thou art an
offence unto me: for thou savourest not the things that be
of God, but those that be of men.'

Thoughts exist on two opposing levels. There are the
thoughts of God and the thoughts of men. The high and
the low, as God said in Isaiah 55:8–9. Satan thinks as men
think. The fact is, Satan simply cannot glimpse God's
outlook at all. That is strange when you remember that he
was originally Lucifer, a throne angel of God. Jesus
bruised the serpent's head, and I think He inflicted some
kind of brain damage upon the Devil! He is disorientated.
Once Satan was full of wisdom, but today that prince of
the power of the air is baffled by what God is doing, and
especially by what the Lord did at the cross. This type of
confusion is brought on by sin.

Men think as the Devil thinks. They too find the cross
foolishness and cannot grasp the things of God, as Paul
remarked. Paul also could not 'see' it at first. Cold fury
against the believers ate away in his heart. He was a
'dragon man', breathing out threats and slaughter. Full of

zeal, his brain was full of clever unbelief. But when he believed, scales fell from his eyes.

I wonder if hell would like to send espionage agents into the kingdom of God, just to see what secrets are there? The demons wouldn't understand these secrets, anyway. Hell is completely baffled. To Satan, Christ's sacrifice is a deep-laid plot devised by God for His own advantage. The Devil devours others. That is his evil nature.

If we were to fight the Devil on the level of human thought, we must remember that he thinks as men think. Satan invented a human chess game and has played this game throughout human history. The Devil anticipates our every move, and he will checkmate us ten miles ahead. Satan has experience from the time of Adam onwards, and he knows every trick of human ingenuity on the board. You cannot produce faith by the wisdom of words. The Devil always has a counter-statement for whatever you say.

The gospel didn't come out of somebody's head. A university professor didn't give it to us. We have to move into the divine dimension, as there the Enemy cannot follow us. The Devil is no match for the mind of the Holy Spirit. If we plan, preach, witness and evangelise as men, Satan will foil us. He can handle psychology and propaganda. The answer is—move in the Spirit and preach the gospel as it is. Then the arch-confuser becomes confused. Then he can't follow the game at all. The Devil doesn't even know the Holy Spirit's alphabet.

We see this constantly in our gospel crusades. We open the meetings to the Holy Spirit completely. The results are thrilling. Whole countries are challenged by the mighty power of Christ. Where false religion and doctrines of demons previously have prevailed, they are shaken and broken. No preacher could do this, no matter how popular or clever. Such success happens only when God does it His way. When He enters the field, there is a mighty victory. He can, will and does succeed—*every time* we allow Him to take over.

These breakthroughs are part of the end-time blessings the Lord promised. The Day of Pentecost continued—it did not stop at Jerusalem, but is for 'the uttermost part of the earth'. I offer this challenge: let anybody begin operating on the level of the Spirit, and they will then see the salvation of the Lord. That kind of evangelism will break Satan's back worldwide, and he will be routed. It is this holy fire which cannot be imitated.

Live ammunition and steam up

When a gun is loaded with blanks, the bang and the recoil are exactly the same as they would be with live ammunition. A difference can be observed in the use of live ammunition and blanks, but not in the noise. The dummy ammunition makes no mark on the target, because it never reaches it. The real bullet can hit its mark. We are not interested in mere bang and recoil, excitement and spectacular gospel displays, even if those might draw hundreds of thousands. We want to see something live hit the bull's-eye. The crowds may come, but we must let loose a true broadside of Holy Spirit fire power in order for something to be accomplished. Multitudes are born again, lives are completely changed, churches are filled, hell is plundered and heaven is populated. Hallelujah!

The fire of God is not sent just for the enjoyment of a few emotional experiences. Praise God, though, the fire of God has that glorious side effect. Holy Ghost power produces lively meetings. But just being happy-clappy does not satisfy God's design. The Holy Spirit works for eternal purposes.

I think of this when I see an old steam engine puffing away. These iron horses are like living creatures, breathing steam with fire in their bellies. The fireman's job is to stoke the fire and get a full head of steam going. When the steam pressure is up, the driver can do one of two things. He can either pull the whistle lever, or he can turn the lever that directs power onto the pistons. The whistle will blow off steam until there's none left, making itself heard for miles around. If power is directed onto the pistons, however, the steam can turn the wheels with far less fuss, drawing no attention to itself. The train then rolls away, carrying its load across the land. Thank God for the train whistle. It is important. But if blowing a whistle was all the steam could do, making a fire under the boiler and stoking it up wouldn't be worth while.

The fire of the Holy Spirit brings power. Never mind the noise—let us apply this power to get on the move. Thunder is justified after lightning has first struck. The proper purpose of Pentecost is to get the wheels rolling for God in every church, thereby transporting the gospel across the face of the whole earth.

'Go ye into all the world and preach the gospel to every creature.' The church is a 'go' church, not a 'sit' church. Look *outwards*, to where our Lord is moving across the continents. Some are looking inwards, everlastingly examining their own souls, incapacitated by introspection. Jesus is saving you—don't you worry. Now start helping Him to save others. If the Holy Ghost has come, then be up and going. He does the work, not you or I. 'Woe is me if I preach not the gospel.' And woe to them to whom we fail to preach it!

The Christian age is the fire age

Let me ask a question. Why was Jesus exalted to the right hand of God? In even the greatest of commentaries, far too little is written about this. Christ's ascension seems to be a neglected study. Is it of such little importance? Jesus declared His ascension to be *expedient* (Jn 16:7). He told us that unless He went to the Father a most essential experience would never be ours. Without the Lord's ascension, we could never be baptised into the Spirit.

Look back upon all that Jesus did. John writes that His works were so many that if they were all written, the whole world could not contain the books. So, what could there be that He did not do when He was on earth? There was one thing. It was the very thing which John the Baptist said He would do—baptise in fire and in the Holy Spirit. He didn't do that when He was on earth. Jesus came from heaven and had to return there, via the cross and the tomb, before the final part of His mission could begin.

Nothing Jesus did on earth could be described as baptising with the Holy Spirit and with fire. In none of His mighty works—His preaching, His teaching, His healing, or in His death and resurrection—did He baptise with the Holy Spirit. Jesus did much for His disciples. He gave them authority to carry out healing missions, but He went away without baptising them into the Holy Ghost.

Such a baptism could not have happened until He went to the Father. Indeed, the Lord not only said it but He emphasised it. *He entered glory to take up this brand new office*, the office of the Baptiser into the Holy Spirit. This is the reason He ascended to the Father. The Old Testament knows nothing of such a baptism. It is God's 'new thing'. Jesus brings us many other blessings now, of course. He is our High Priest, our Advocate, our Representative. But He did not name these works. He only described the sending forth of the Spirit.

When He did ascend, and not before, the Spirit came and 'cloven tongues like as of fire sat upon each of them'. The altars of the Tabernacle of Moses and the Temple of Solomon had been set ablaze by the pure fire from heaven. The flames in the Upper Room of Pentecost then came from the same heavenly source. Jesus has all power at His command. He is in the control room.

Tongues of fire

If baptising into the Holy Spirit is His work, it means that everything to do with Him and with the gospel should be characterised by fire. It should burn. There should be fire in those who witness and work. Fire in those who preach. Fire in the truth we preach—'Is not my word like as a fire?' (Jer 23:29). Fire in the Lord we preach—'Our God is a consuming fire' (Heb 12:29). Fire in the power to preach—'Tongues like as of fire' (Acts 2:3). Fire in the Spirit by which we preach—'With the Holy Ghost and with fire' (Mt 3:11).

Now let me show you some things which are very important:

1. All sacrifice must be consumed by fire

There were two sacrifices on Mount Carmel. One was performed by the priests of Baal, the other by Elijah. The first one, the sacrifice to Baal, never burned. It was fireless. The sacrifice was there. The sacrificers were intensely earnest. They prayed to Baal all day, and they lanced themselves with knives to show how desperate their sincerity was. They put everything they had into it, and yet their sacrifice brought no fire. If the Devil could have brought up a spark or two from hell to make a blaze, he would have, but the altar just stayed cold.

Fire did not fall just because Elijah set up a sacrifice. It came when Elijah prayed and believed. 'Faith is victory.' Elijah set everything up as he should, that is true. He followed the instructions of Moses to the letter, but no fire resulted purely from his obedience. Faith brought the blaze.

God sent the fire on the sacrifice only. There would be no point in sending the fire without the sacrifice. Armchair Christians receive no fire. Sometimes people pray for fire when they are simply not yielded to God at all, and subsequently do little for Him. They give up little time or money, and render no effort. If they had God's fire, what would they do with it? Sit at home and just enjoy it? The fire is not to save us trouble in winning the world—it is for those who take the trouble to preach the gospel.

It is the fire that matters. Laying out and setting up a sacrifice is not enough. God won't save souls and heal the sick until we lay our all on the altar for Him—that is true. But our sacrifice is not *why* He does it. He performs His

wonders of salvation and healing because of His mercy
and grace. Elijah's godliness did not generate the awesome lightning that burned up everything on the altar.
The fire did not come from his holiness. Your tithes and
offerings cannot buy a tiny candle flame of the celestial
flame. The fire of God comes, not because of our sacrifice,
but because of Christ's sacrifice. Therefore, thank God,
the fire is for all. Revival fire is not a reward for good
people. It is God's gift. Why struggle for it? People talk
about 'paying the price'. But it is a case of 'you pay a great
deal too dear for what's given freely'. Fire comes by faith.

2. Truth needs to be fire-baptised

We can be dead right, but dead nonetheless. We can insist
on the 'body of truth', but it may be a cold corpse. Jesus
did not merely say, 'I am the way and the truth.' He is the
life as well. God said He would put in Zion 'the shining of
a flaming fire' (Is 4:5). Jesus testified that John the Baptist
was a 'burning and shining light' (Jn 5:35). Images of
light and heat. The gospel is a hot gospel, however much
the silly world smiles at it.

I do not know how to preach the 'lively oracles' of God
(Acts 7:38) without being lively. The gospel is about fire.
To preach the gospel coolly and casually would be
ridiculous. One day a lady told me that there was a
'demon' sitting on her, although she was a born-again
Christian. I said to her, 'Flies can only sit on a cold stove,
and on a cold stove they can sit a long time! Get the fire of
the Holy Spirit into your life, and that dirty demon will
not dare to touch you, in case he burns his filthy fingers.'
The gospel provides its own fiery power. It is natural,
therefore, for a preacher to be fired-up.

In human experience, God's fire translates into passion, the type of passion we saw in Jesus. Perhaps He
wasn't always passionate in His words. When Jesus was
going to Jerusalem for the last time, we read that He was
walking ahead of His disciples. They saw how He urged
Himself onwards. 'They were in the way going up to

Jerusalem; and Jesus went before them: and they were amazed; and as they followed they were afraid' (Mk 10:32). Why? Somehow, the fires in His soul were evident in the way He walked.

When they arrived, Jesus saw the desecration of the Temple. The disciples then had further evidence of His passionate feeling. His reaction turned Him into an awesome figure. The disciples were reminded of the words of Psalm 69:9: 'The zeal of thine house hath eaten me up.' But it was a love anger, not a cold fury. Jesus wasn't a frenzied fanatic. He loved His Father's house, that's all. It was His desire to see people in the Temple, worshipping with freedom and happiness. But commercialism in the temple had spoiled all that. His heart overflowed like a volcano. The fire in His soul made Him cleanse the Temple. His actions were frightening, and many fled from the scene because of them. The children, the blind and the lame stayed, though, and He healed them.

That was what He had wanted to do, anyway, and that was the reason His anger achieved furnace heat. His indignation aimed for joy. Jesus got the children singing, 'Hosanna!' This was the only occasion in Scripture where excitement about God was rebuked; the only time a hush was demanded in the courts of the Lord. The silence was demanded by the Pharisees—the praise of the Lord was drowning the tinkling of their commercial tills. Money music was muted. This was all part of the picture of the fire of the Lord.

A museum of marble figures

A burning message, *and nothing but that,* was supposed to be presented to the world. There doesn't have to be fireworks. Firebrands don't need to be hotheads. Everything about the church, however, should reflect the warm light of God, to the very highest steeple. 'Everything in his temple cries Glory.' We read that God makes His ministers 'a flame of fire' (Heb 1:7). His people should be torches. Not only evangelists, but witnesses, ministers, church officials, leaders, workers, teachers and administrators should all glow with the Holy Ghost, like torches in a cold street. The business meeting should see Holy Spirit fire just as much as the revival meeting—perhaps even more so.

A fish has the same temperature as the water in which it swims. Too many Christians are like fish—they have no more warmth of spirit than the cold, unbelieving world around them. Men are warm-blooded creatures. That is the way the Lord made us. That is also the way He chose us to take the good news—with warmth!

The Lord does not send us out because we have cool heads and dignity. Nor does He choose us for our self-composure. He sends us out with live coals from the altar, as witnesses to the Resurrection, to testify that we have met the God of Pentecost. I've heard sermons that were like lectures on embalming the dead. Would such a talk remind anyone of the living Jesus? Neither Jesus, Peter nor Paul left congregations sitting like marble statues in a museum.

Logic can be set alight and still be logic, like the logic of Isaiah or Paul, for example. Logic need not belong to the glacial period. Fire implies fervour, not ignorance. Learn, by all means, but not if it puts the fire out. Remember—radiance before cleverness. 'Thou shalt love the Lord thy God with all thine heart, mind, soul and strength.' The Lord wants us to have a warm heart, joy, gusto and love.

Human dignity takes on a new meaning when people are rapt in praise to God. Have you ever seen 50,000 people weeping, waving, jumping and shouting in gladness to God? What else would you expect to happen when a mother stands on our platform, testifying that her child has just been healed of congenital blindness or deafness, or perhaps of twisted limbs? I have seen these miracle testimonies so often. It is a glorious scene, the height of human experience.

It is not to our credit when we keep perfectly cool as the

lame walk and the blind see. Such reserve isn't clever—it is stupid. Dance—that's more in keeping with such moments. Joy in the presence of the Lord. Jesus said that at such times even the stones would cry out.

I look at the precious men and women, black or white, many who were so sad earlier, standing in a meeting, hands pressed together in emotion or lifted in worship, eyes glistening with glad tears, faces turned up to God, lips moving in wondering thankfulness. I say to myself, 'How beautiful they are!' In such moments, I wish I were an artist. When so-called dignity comes before our delight in God, that is a catastrophe.

If God does not touch our feelings, the Devil will. How can God convict sinners and help them come to repentance unless they feel moved? How can He grant them the joy of sins forgiven without giving them any sensation in their souls? *I believe an evangelist's job is to light a fire in the human spirit.*

Getting folk saved is more than getting their names on a dotted line. Christianity isn't a club they are joining. Salvation is spiritual surgery. What is the forgiveness which we proclaim? What sort of forgiveness did Jesus give? It was the real kind of mercy. This forgiveness made a cripple walk again, and it melted a street woman's hardness enough to cause her to wash His feet with tears. It was the sort of forgiveness which made people love much. It was the kind which made them do something extravagant, like throw a party as Levi did. This forgiveness caused Mary to break open a box of spikenard worth a small fortune, and Zacchaeus to give away lots of money.

The disciples were crazy with joy when they cast out devils, but Jesus said that was nothing. 'Rejoice not, that the spirits are subject unto you; but rather rejoice, because your names are written in heaven. In that hour Jesus rejoiced in spirit' (Lk 10:20–21).

Peter heard Him say those words, and He took in that lesson. Later Peter wrote this about believers: 'Whom having not seen, ye love; in whom, though now ye see him not, yet believing, ye rejoice with joy unspeakable and full of glory: Receiving the end of your faith, even the salvation of your souls' (1 Pet 1:8–9).

Rejoice in undertones? Worship in whispers? Participate in silent celebrations? That is not what the word 'rejoice' means in this scripture. It means 'to exult, shout, be rapturous'. Try doing that without emotion, without fire!

The fire of the Holy Spirit is for real. It must flow through the church of Jesus Christ like blood through the veins. God's people on fire, and the church as a whole on fire, will win our lost generation for Him.

2

The Anti-Anointed

How long can the last hour last?

Suppose it was your last hour. What would you be doing? What a flurry of anxious preparations there would be. But let me tell you, it *is* the last hour.

'Children, it is the last hour' (1 Jn 2:18 RSV). I know it seems that this hour has lasted a very long time as John wrote those words 1,900 years ago. But don't let that fact confuse you. Of one thing we can be certain—if it was the last hour then, it most certainly is now! We could rewrite this text today to read, 'Little children, it is the last second of the last hour.'

When John wrote this verse, he was watching God's clock, not ours. Its hands have not stood still. How long will God's hour last, measured by earthly time-keeping methods? The one thing we know is that we *don't* know how near we are to the end. 'But of that day and hour knoweth no man,' Jesus said in Matthew 24:36. It is obvious, however, that we are much closer to the end every day. Paul saw it that way too: 'Knowing the time,

that now it is high time to awake out of sleep: for now is
our salvation nearer than when we believed' (Rom 13:11).

If anybody thought they had only sixty minutes left,
they would certainly not spend the time on trivialities.
With the sands running out, we would see what was really
important to them. They would not go shopping for the
latest fashionable hat, or run an eye down the financial
columns to see how their shares were doing. Focusing on
the end would put all of life into its proper perspective.

Somebody once said that most people live as if this life
were a permanent arrangement. The Bible's message is
that our days are 'numbered'—not numberless. There is
actually only time for the important things. I am thinking
about the church of Jesus Christ in particular. People
often point out that life consists of a thousand details, but
minors must not outweigh majors. The church has one
aim to concern itself with—the war with Satan and the
campaign for souls.

The great quality of Jesus is that He came when the
Father sent Him. And the great quality about us should be
that we go when Jesus sends us. 'As my Father hath sent
me, even so send I you' (Jn 20:21). The church should
plan to neglect anything which interferes with going.

Last-hour logic

When Scripture proclaims, 'It is the last hour...', it truly
is. For the message of the gospel, *it is always the last hour*.
God has been fair and righteous to all generations. This is
the unique and special doctrine of Scripture called 'immi-
nence'.

Many ease back into thinking, 'There's still four
months to harvest.' If you want to know how a single
individual like Paul did so much, read his disclosure in 1
Corinthians 7:29–31 (New International Version). He
lived as if the end of all things was at hand, as if the final
curtain were always imminent.

What I mean, brothers, is that the time is short. From now on those who have wives should live as if they had none; those who mourn, as if they did not; those who are happy, as if they were not; those who buy something, as if it were not theirs to keep; those who use the things of the world, as if not engrossed in them. For this world in its present form is passing away.

The gospel is eternal, but we haven't eternity to preach it. We could think we had that long if we viewed the often leisurely operations of the church on the gospel front. We have only as long as we live to reach those who live as long as we live. At present, over five billion souls are living. These are living in our present world, not in an indefinite future age which needs to be evangelised. It is the last hour.

Run!

To make sure the Prodigal Son was welcomed home properly, the father ran! Ran! I have wanted to run, too, since the Holy Spirit charged my soul with this realisation—'It is the last hour.' The world's airlines have found me to be a good customer. One of Paul's favourite Greek words was *spoude*, meaning 'to stretch out the neck as a man running to get to the winning post'. It is translated 'be diligent, study, be earnest, hasten, be zealous, be forward'.

Many churches are very active, but active doing what? To fiddle about with secular issues is one way to look impressively busy and 'relevant'. But to bring the gospel to a dying world is the mark of true relevance. The world must be made relevant to the gospel, or perish.

Giving all our thoughts to our personal spirituality, when the fires of hell have broken out, is like members of the fire brigade having a shave before answering a fire call. We can spend years 'standing for our principles' when we are only justifying our church quarrels and prejudices. The command to evangelise is all that matters; snatching men from the flames.

That divine command was not given in a passing mood

of the Lord. God Himself is driven by the peril in which human beings stand without Christ. Calvary was His imperative. 'Other sheep I have... them also I must bring' (Jn 10:16). Jesus told the disciples on the Emmaus road that it 'behoved Christ to suffer'. The same Greek word, *dei*, is used in both these sayings of Christ. The word does not mean that it was fitting or proper for Him to suffer, but that He *had* to do so—that it was in Him to do it. The God who went to the lengths of the cross did not do so to give us a hobby or an interest for our leisure time. Our Lord did not die to provide a minor occupation for a few church folk. He commands us to preach the gospel to every creature. This task *needs* us all.

We would deceive ourselves, and lose the inner meaning of the word of God, if we were to think that this 'last hour' were not upon us. It is! It is no use saying, 'God's last hour is a pretty long one, so why hurry?' We only have today. In the most intense meaning of the word, it *is* the last hour. John may have written it long centuries ago, but he was right. There was no hiccup in his inspiration.

It is the last hour for somebody whose toecaps already hang over the abyss of eternity.

It is the last hour of opportunity in many a place.

It is the last hour of possibility to obey the command of the Lord when He said: 'Go ye into all the world....'

It is the last hour before Jesus returns.

Paid by the hour

Years ago, in northern Germany, I had the privilege of leading an elderly lady to the Lord. For most of her life she had been a church organist, but yet had never known Jesus as her own Saviour. When she heard the gospel and opened her heart to the Lord, she was overwhelmed with the joy of the Holy Spirit. Three days later I met her again, but this time she was completely broken. Puzzled, I asked her why this was. With tears in her eyes, she told me. 'I am already seventy years of age and have only just received Jesus as my Saviour. I may live perhaps another five or ten years, but I have totally wasted seventy.'

Of course, this touched me deeply. Then I said, 'Yes, but I know what is going to happen. One day we shall stand before the judgement seat of Christ. But He will not be as concerned about *how long* we cut the furrow of our life for Him, as *how deep*. Five or ten years out and out for Jesus, are better than having been a lukewarm Christian for fifty years.'

Do you remember the labourers of the parable of Jesus? By the clock, some had worked only a single hour, but the farmer generously rewarded them, paying them the same as those who had laboured throughout the day. Why? Because they had worked as long as they had the chance to work. This is the principle of God.

If anybody is worried about not having been at Jesus' side in the harvest when they could have been, the answer is to leave that with the Lord of the harvest. Don't waste the remaining time on tears. Give God, from this moment on, wholeheartedly what is His due! The apostle Paul's advice is this: go flat out for the mark of the prize of the high calling in Christ, and forget those things which are behind (Phil 3:13–14). As long as you have breath within you, you are in time to be in on the last hour, the last day, the last month or the last year. You are not too late for that.

Young people have a slightly different status in the same last hour, however. When an old person is saved, a soul is saved. When a young person is saved, both a soul *and* a lifetime are saved. The young person has an hour which could be a lifetime, and what a glorious hour that can be! An hour full of love, joy, peace, purpose and security, even if the last hour lasted an entire lifetime. The only way to live tomorrow is to live in faith and activity for Jesus today.

I once prayed for an old and dying man. Suddenly, a strange thought challenged me: 'What would you pray if you were in his place?' A famous politician who expressed his last wish asked for 'one of Bellamy's pork pies'! It didn't take long before I knew the answer for myself. I would ask the Lord to give me the strength and help to conduct one more gospel crusade! I would like to hit the bull's-eye once more; once more to lead 100,000 souls to the foot of the cross. There is nothing grander than that, nor is there a more glorious way to die, than fighting on that victorious battle ground.

Glorious crescendo

The thought of the year 2,000 was much in the minds of nineteenth-century believers. For them, the coming of the twentieth century strongly suggested Christ's soon return. These Christians prayed for new power to evangelise the world within 100 years. The goal of world evangelisation was often on their minds, and the thought filled them with much longing. God heard.

Marine scientists tell us that ocean waves travel thousands of miles, even under the surface and across apparent calm stretches. Approaching land, they develop a majestic crescendo, hunch their mighty shoulders, and build up in rapid momentum and volume to burst finally and magnificently upon the shore.

A glorious swell of Holy Ghost power is gathering to a spontaneous crescendo today, world wide, as if hurrying to the shore. The lifting of the waves proves that the shore cannot be far. Jesus is coming soon! IT IS THE LAST HOUR!

The latter day Pentecostal outpouring of the Spirit began in 1901 and the truth of the Baptism in the Holy Spirit was recovered with signs following. The mightiest revival of all time has swept onwards ever since like a wave from heaven. It was the same tidal wave which had started in Jerusalem 1900 years before. A divine deluge of power, 'floods upon the dry ground' had blessed the world for two or three hundred years.

Then through unbelief and worldliness it seemed to peter out. The church even taught that such power was

only for the apostles and the early disciples. As if only they
needed it! The Holy Ghost became a mere Third Article of
the creed, locked up and relegated to the past.

Anointed for the last hour

With this wonderful outpouring of His Spirit, the Lord
gave believers the power to do the job. The first tasks
God's people did were to evangelise and to send out
missionaries.

This fulfils John's statement in 1 John, a statement in
which he writes of the 'last hour':

> Little children, it is the last hour: and as ye have heard that
> antichrist shall come, even now are there many antichrists;
> whereby we know that it is the last time...But ye have an
> unction [anointing] from the Holy One...Who is a liar but he
> that denieth that Jesus is the Christ? He is antichrist...But
> the anointing which ye have received of him abideth in you (1
> Jn 2:18–27).

The church is being anointed for the last hour. The
spirit of the age would be anti-Christ, or anti-anointed.
The anointing of the Holy Spirit is a theme which threads
its way through that first book of John. The apostle's
warnings concerning the last times have come home to us
today. They strike us with almost frightening accuracy
about our times. The spirit of anti-christ permeates
human thinking and society. This spirit is causing moral
collapse. Hostile elements are raging worse and worse, like
the early moments of a gathering storm. It is indeed the
last hour.

God has His answer, however—the anointing for an
anti-anointed latter day. He will never allow the Devil to
get the upper hand. The outpouring of the Spirit is His
special provision for the last hour. 'It shall come to pass
afterward, that I will pour out my spirit upon all
flesh...before the great and the terrible day of the Lord
come' (Joel 2:28–31). Christ's whole body on earth will be

mobilised and armed for the last onslaught of the Enemy. The Devil will lose again. Satan is the eternal loser.

Bible prophecies are history in advance

This is the time of ripening for the final harvest. Both wheat and tares fill the field. Satan can see his opportunities are slipping away—it is now or never for him. So the greatest display of wickedness, lawlessness and degradation is ahead. But believers have more to think about than mere survival. There are likely to be persecutions, and no doubt blood will flow. Our thoughts, however, are on triumph and conquest for Jesus. The build-up of enemy forces is being more than matched by an ever-increasing measure of the Holy Spirit. 'When the enemy shall come in like a flood, the spirit of the Lord shall lift up a standard against him' (Is 59:19).

The greatest outpouring, the greatest anointing of God's power ever known, is coming upon us. Past revivals will seem as nothing when Pentecost breaks upon the entire church. We get glimpses of it already—the battle of the anointed against the anti-anointed. We now know what it means in Revelation 12:11: 'And they overcame him by the blood of the Lamb, and by the word of their testimony; and they loved not their lives unto death.' That showdown is fully described in Revelation 12:9–10:

> And the great dragon was cast out, that old serpent, called the Devil and Satan, which deceiveth the whole world: he was cast out into the earth, and his angels were cast out with him. And I heard a loud voice saying in heaven, Now is come salvation, and strength, and the kingdom of our God, and the power of his Christ: for the accuser of our brethren is cast down.

Bible prophecies like these are not alterable. They are history written in advance. When the Devil is out to trouble the world, God will trouble the Devil. God will do what He said He would, even to the dot on the last 'i'.

Hallelujah! We rejoice. We know. The future is settled beforehand, and the last hour is determined, with its very glorious conclusion. And this is the period we now are entering into!

In our great African gospel crusades, there are victories over satanic powers and over sorcery. Gigantic piles of witchcraft materials are brought together and burned. Their owners have been delivered from satanic fears and oppressions by receiving Jesus as their Lord and Saviour. I often have pointed to the flames, saying to the crowds, 'That is like where the final home of the Devil will be, in the lake of fire!' Satan is not in control of hell's fire—those flames are his judgement. When those 'works of the devil' are reduced to ashes, we then see the true fire of the Lord fall on crowds 'en masse'. Nothing of the old serpent is then left.

The anti-anointing is a strange fire of destruction and of death. But the flame from the presence of the Lord will devour it, just as it devoured the strange fire of Nadab and Abihu. After that, a sweet anointing of peace shall flow over the church, all the way down to its feet and robe hems.

Let us forget old fights among God's people over issues which do not lead to the salvation of men and women. Our enemy is not another denomination. Our enemy is not even denominationalism. Our enemy is the Devil, and the lies by which he deceives the world—the lie that God is dead, the lie that God is indifferent, the lie that we can do without Him. 'They overcame him by the blood of the Lamb.' Note that 'him' is singular. We have one enemy— the Devil. There is one power to oppose him—the anointing of the Holy Spirit. 'The yoke shall be destroyed because of the anointing' (Is 10:27).

3

Immortal Works for Mortals

A man with a mission needs vision. Isaiah and Jeremiah needed theirs. Without their vision, they would never have carried on. To be called by God costs nothing, as God does the calling. To birth the call is another matter entirely. A man would give up unless he were called.

I was a hard-working missionary in Lesotho, but the dream of a blood-washed Africa haunted me. The vision became more persistent and vivid. An all-consuming desire drove me to make my first ventures. But I was still hesitant. The members of the mission board disapproved, good and spiritual men that they were. Karl Barth wrote, 'Faith is never identical with piety.' Normal missionary work was the fruitful approach to the salvation of Africa they believed, not mass evangelism. Why did I think I could do it differently? If this was God's way, why were other men not doing it? Missionaries were content with the mission tradition—were they wrong and was I right?

I felt isolated. Then I met with a group of evangelists for fellowship, and everyone had a story to tell that was similar to mine. They shared a common experience of official discouragement. They had the burning fire of the Spirit within, the challenge of vast possibilities around, but criticism from without. During these birth pangs, many times in agony of mind, I had to spend hours in prayer to keep my poise and peace. How long would it take to bring about a blood-washed Africa without aggressive evangelistic crusades? We have only one generation to save a generation. Every generation needs regeneration.

The pressure reached a crisis point. One day I locked myself in a hotel room in Lesotho to pray. I was determined that I would not let God go until I had a clear word from Him. I boldly put before the Lord exactly how I felt and said that I was sick and tired of the strain— constrained to evangelise, but restrained by men. Was this really His will for me, this constant impulse to campaign? Other workers did not seem to believe mass evangelism was a good course of action.

That day God made matters clear to me. As frankly as I had spoken to the Lord, He spoke in reply. He said, 'If you drop the vision which I have given you, I shall have to look for another man who will accept it and do what I want.'

I repented of my hesitations immediately. I made my decision, for ever. God then began to smile upon me and give me divine encouragement. Since that day, I have not looked back. I learned how to handle critics and their criticisms by letting God Himself become my Defender. Let them see the Lord had led me by the fruit which it bears, I decided. I concentrated on what He wanted me to do and the ministry and the results grew—step by step, dimension to dimension, sometimes rather dramatically.

'Curiously wrought'

Evangelism happens to be my calling. There are other callings which will grip men and women. Apostles, pastors, teachers, prophets, elders, musicians, organisers, intercessors, workers in a thousand different capacities. When God puts His hand upon us, He does two things.

First, He gives us a ministry, then He opens a door to service. Each one of us has a unique and vital place in His temple. Every believer is individually chiselled, 'curiously wrought in the lowest parts of the earth', as Psalm 139 puts it. Some are far from being run-of-the-mill. They are hardly likely to be welcomed with a great cheer.

A new vision can be disturbing, not only to those who have it, but to those who don't, especially if it puts a man in the limelight. There can be resentment, criticism, even jealousy. Sometimes a man's close friends and colleagues can't believe God has put a call into his soul. There is no accounting for God's choice, as Paul points out about Jacob. If God calls, the best proof is our patience when we are misjudged and criticised. The man who knows God has sent him will rest in God, and leave those who disapprove for the Lord to handle. 'Humble yourselves therefore under the mighty hand of God, that he may exalt you in due time.'

One must be careful not to mishandle criticisms. Sometimes, through the eyes of others, you see the back of your own head. What others say about us is important, be they enemies or friends. I praise the Lord for those choice men and women to whom the Lord has guided me, with their perception and insight. I would be a fool not to listen to them. Of course evangelists need advice. The evangelist cannot be a law unto himself. He is a member of the body of Christ.

Dan, the shipowner

It is marvellous how the word of God stirs us. Judges 5:16–20 did this for me, unexpectedly, in a unique way the Lord interpreted it in my thoughts.

Let me remind you first that, in the period of the Judges, Israel had many ups and downs. Often the people were oppressed by invaders. God then would raise up charismatic leaders to unite them and to help them to defend themselves. One of these judges was a woman,

Deborah, who was a prophetess. In her day, a Canaanite king, Jabin, sent in his men, plundering and killing, under Sisera.

Deborah was stirred to resist by the Spirit of God. However, she was no Joan of Arc, and did not deck herself in armour to fight like a man. She used her persuasive powers to inspire the men of Israel to rally their tribes under the leadership of Barak.

Each tribe received her call to unite and do what they could not do alone, standing against Sisera. Some came, some did not. It is very interesting to see how the various tribes reacted. In fact, this old story is like a mirror held up to the face of the church today.

Ship shops

Scrutinising Israel after victory had come, Deborah asked one penetrating question about the tribe of Dan—'Why did Dan remain in ships?' (Judg 5:17). The Danites were merchants, running a kind of mercantile marine service for Israel. They brought in goods from the far corners of the earth. Then, moored in a harbour, the ships became shops, selling directly from the importer to the public.

Now here is how I picture it. Dan himself is at the till of his shop. The day has been great, and profits are good. He is reckoning everything up with satisfaction. Then, a sudden disturbance on the harbour side distracts him. A messenger arrives, exhausted from the urgent run, carrying a letter to Dan. It reads:

Dear Dan,

Jabin, the King of Canaan, has sent Sisera and is harrying Israel. We are fighting with everything at our disposal, but we need help. The tribes must all unite to repel the enemy. Come and help—*now*. Your fellow Israelites are bleeding and dying. Please respond. Come at once!

Greetings,

DEBORAH (Judge of Israel)

Dan, the businessman, was deeply moved. He jumped up and looked inland, where he thought hostilities might be in progress. He possibly heard the clash of arms and the cries of his dying brothers. But then, just as suddenly, he was moved by other thoughts. Awfully worrying questions troubled him. Could he just leave his money, uncounted? If he went and fought, what would happen to his ships and shops? Wouldn't he be risking his flourishing enterprise? And there was something else. Canaanites were his customers. He must not upset them. Shouldn't he remain neutral? What if his ships sank while he neglected them while enlisting in the army?

After such considerations, he decided. Hurriedly, he stuffed a bundle of money into the messenger's pockets and said, 'I certainly want to help. Regretfully, I can't come myself, but here's my contribution. Tell Deborah I'm with her in spirit.'

Wonderful man, to let the women do the fighting! So Dan went on counting his cash while his brethren rallied round the standard of Deborah and Barak. Let others die for Israel, but Dan had a business to attend to. There was Dan in his ship—the ship of self-interest, self-love and greed.

Who does Dan represent today? It is for each one of us to ask ourselves. Dan is the Christian who belongs to the family of God, knows what the claims of God upon him are, hears the call of God, but does not respond to it. He remains in his ship shop when God wants him to 'seek first the kingdom of God'. The music of the tinkling till, the applause of the unconverted or the opinion of family and friends deafen him to the call of the living God.

In church he sings about the sweet bye and bye on the golden shore, but will his ship reach it, or just flounder in the sea of life? If you think such situations could not be, just look around. See the wreckage of lives where people have chosen the wrong priorities. Some of the saddest people have been those with an eye to the main chance, who didn't keep their eyes on God. They lost their vision.

Things went terribly wrong in the end. Success turned to ashes, popularity went sour. They chose the Danite opportunities of the ship shop. They let others follow Christ to His harvest field, or battlefield, or maybe mission field, and at the last saw their joy and contentment, realising their own tragedy. 'Summer is ended, harvest is over and we are not saved.'

Makers of money—or history?

The runner with Deborah's letter hoped for a better response as he reached Zebulun and Naphtali. The two men were working in the fields and in the villages under the warm sun. The younger and fitter men were looking forward to the end of the day and to the joy of their young wives and children. They got together around the dispatch runner to hear and consider Deborah's call to service. What should they do? Why, there was only one choice— go! 'Praise the Lord,' they said, 'that the Lord has anointed somebody to lead us. Now, let's make an end of this constant harassment from Jabin and his bandits. Thank God for Deborah! We'll back her to the hilt. Tell her we're on the way. Count on us.'

They exchanged their pruning hooks for spears. Children were hugged, weeping wives kissed, and the men marched away into the dust of battle. 'Zebulun and Naphtali were a people that jeoparded their lives unto the death in the high places of the field' (Judg 5:18).

The war was soon won. But it brought no glory to Dan. Deborah, a woman, had led Israel, and another woman, Jael wife of Heber, struck the famous final blow. She pinned Sisera to the ground in her own tent with a peg through his head, ending the rampage of his Canaanite army.

Deborah then went on her judge's rounds and arrived at the harbour quayside to visit Dan. She only wanted to ask him one withering question—'Why did Dan remain in his ship?' Dan sat still, his fingers fumbling nervously with a coin. He couldn't lift his eyes to face this Holy Ghost-anointed woman of God. Her question haunted him for the rest of his life. That question will be heard again at the throne of God, when Dan and all the rest of us have to give account for our lives. Will Dan look at the Lord? Or will he be too ashamed, not knowing what to answer, hanging his head in confusion?

Zebulun and Naphtali did not have the eye for business Dan did—Dan was smarter. Dan made money. But Zebulun and Naphtali made history that day, fighting and winning to save Israel in a remarkable battle still talked about 3,000 years later. They risked everything, even life itself, fighting in the high places of the field. Dan staked nothing. He never took risks. When Dan died, he was the richest and yet most miserable man in the country, with bars of gold in his bedroom right to the ceiling, constantly within view so he could gloat about it. Dan had lived for gold for so long. Then, as his soul was leaving his body, Dan grabbed for his gold, wanting to take it with him. The angel of death swept him away, though, with a laugh. 'You've made your pile, and now somebody else will spend it,' the angel declared.

The call of God is heard by Zebulun and Naphtali people today, but not by the Dan people. Churches are composed of one or the other kind of people. The Dan people are those who consider their businesses more important than God's work; their back gardens more important than the harvest fields; their homes more important than heaven for the lost; saving money more important than saving souls. 'I have married a wife and cannot come.' Zebulun left his wife, though, and saved the kingdom.

Ask any pastor, and he will tell you who are the Dan or the Zebulun and Naphtali characters. 'It's always the same people who respond, and give, and work. If it weren't for them, this church would close.' Some obey God's call at any cost, but others would not risk £5 for

God. Zebulun and Naphtali died on the high places of the battle ground for God and for God's kingdom.

Jesus said, 'He that shall lose his life shall find it,' and, 'Be thou faithful unto death, and I will give thee the crown of life.' There's a nobility in that kind of dying, and even in a person's readiness to give all, which we now recognise and honour on earth. But the Lord Himself will recognise it when a glittering crown of life is placed upon his head by the hand of Christ Himself. Of the Dan folk, Jesus said, 'He that saveth his life shall lose it.'

That woman!

After the battle came the celebration. Deborah the prophetess and Barak the general sang a victory song, naming the tribes one by one. The song is full of irony. After Dan and Zebulun and Naphtali, they named Reuben, about whom it is written for ever, as if in stone: 'For the divisions of Reuben there were great searchings of heart' (Judg 5:16).

Let me continue to draw my simple picture. The Reuben people were thoughtful types, people of consideration and judgement. They were the educated, the talkers. When the sweating and dusty dispatch runner came panting into their midst shouting, 'Urgent! Urgent! A message from Judge Deborah,' Reuben quickly took the letter. Immediately he called an emergency meeting of the Council of the Wise. Together, they gave Deborah's letter the serious attention they always directed to every issue. The council sat down and first read the minutes of the last meeting. The members pondered the situation. They were keen thinkers. Their perceptions soon showed them it was too big a matter for any rash decision, a decision which might later be regretted. With their usual caution, it was decided that they would sleep on the matter and the council would meet again the next day with fresh minds.

So, the next day, Deborah's call was carefully looked at from every angle. The unanimous conclusion was recorded in their minutes—action was needed. But, a plan had to be drawn up before they rushed into battle. The next day, therefore, a strategy was devised, and general tactics were itemised. Excellent! Now, what about logistics, means, command? Another whole day was gladly devoted to these very important matters. The council would ensure the success of the battle. They would be a first-class army. The planning all took time, but it was better that they go well-prepared.

During that session, they had a tea break and went out to stretch their legs, feeling very content with their work thus far. While strolling, they caught a faint sound of the distant struggle and saw the smoke of burning villages in the sky. A straggler staggered into view, bleeding from his wounds. Thankfully, they felt they were already working on a project to help. Meanwhile, the battle went on.

There was one main difficulty that troubled them. The council met again the following day, and at last had to put the matter on the agenda. The problem was Deborah. She was a woman! How could they consider the call of a mere female? Where were the grounds for that in their Scriptures? When had a woman ever taken the lead—except to lead Adam into sin? Deborah stood between them and action. Their learning and knowledge saw no way to permit themselves to go at her call. The action had no precedent. A female taking authority to govern and to judge? Could God bless men following a woman into battle? It soon became clear to them. Their duty was to decline to go. It was a matter of principle.

This all reflects upon our own day. People often don't like the way things are being done. They don't like the leadership, or the method, or the timing, or the personnel. Sometimes intellectual objections are found. 'Evangelism—what with all our education? This is not the age of Paul and Peter! Soul saving? Revivalism? That was all fine for backwoodsmen, but we need a different approach.' Yet, these people never find a different method.

Some have a gospel of loaves and fishes. Jesus said, 'Labour not for the meat which perisheth, but for the meat which endureth unto everlasting life which the Son of Man shall give unto you' (John 6:27).

There are others more concerned about spirituality and quality than about plucking men from eternal burning. They make fine speeches and adorn the platform in an elegant fashion, but they are absent on the frontlines. Some are ultra-devout, deeply concerned with the work of the Spirit within themselves or in their churches. An evangelist would disturb and interrupt what God has been doing these past years. They can't support evangelists. Evangelists garner attention, and deeper developments are hindered. So, the pious words flow and no effort is made. Precious people go on dying in their sins, just the same.

On holiday

There is another tribe to discuss. The dispatch reaches Asher in the hands of an anxious and exhausted envoy. What happens? 'Asher continued on the sea shore.' Asher was on vacation. 'I'm sorry,' he told the collapsing dispatch carrier, 'I need this rest. I couldn't break off my holiday, now, could I?'

Asher worked very hard in his job and had no time. Church duties were nice for those with nothing else to do, but he had his accounts to see to after business hours, and he owed himself this break without interruption. No, he couldn't come at the moment.

'But,' Asher said, 'I'm sure plenty of others will turn up and help. Some people are cut out for that sort of thing. Deborah will be all right.' Asher sat up in his deckchair and took a long drink. 'Yes, tell her we admire her. She's marvellous, and we have confidence that we can leave the matter in her hands. God won't fail her. We'll be praying and believing for victory. Explain my predicament, that I need to stay here on the beach for a while, or I won't be any good to run my business.'

Depend on others to do what you won't do yourself. This is all too common. 'Somebody will turn up, and it will get done. I like to spend my weekends where I can get away from it all. I have a place in the country, and it would be silly not to go there.' For some, anything they have planned, anything that crops up, any other demand but that of God, and it has prior attention. They can't do all that *and* save souls. That is piling on the work. They need some relaxation at times, and some things have to be attended to. Commitments come first. They will help, sooner or later, when they are free, have nothing else to do and feel up to it.

Well—I visualised that Dan came to his tragic end. And Reuben—what happened to him? I hear that he dropped dead, still talking. He let Deborah down, but the undertaker was the last to let him down. As for Asher, he became overweight and had blood pressure problems because of a lack of exercise. Asher never did a stroke, had a stroke, and died. He lost his life saving it.

That is the parable from the story of Deborah. It remains a solemn matter for consideration in our own lives today. Jesus used humour when He spoke of a camel going through the eye of a needle, as He warned the rich about the difficulty they would have entering the kingdom of God. People do make excuses, like the outrageous examples Christ used in the parable of the wedding feast. The first one to decline the invitation had married a wife. Another had bought land, and yet another one had purchased oxen. They had their pleasures for a time and then lost the crown for ever.

Some in our own CfaN (Christ for all Nations) team already have received that crown. A terrible accident occurred in 1985. We had been to Zaire, and a glorious gospel victory had brought thousands into the kingdom of God in the city of Lubumbashi. As many as 80,000 packed the stadium. Multitudes were reached through the live regional radio and television broadcasts.

After the crusade, our trucks made their way back to Zambia. Across the border, an unknown driver was drinking. He drove his tanker towards our convoy, colliding with one of our CfaN gospel trucks. There was a blaze and two of our CfaN technicians, Horst Kosanke and Milton Kasselman, died. The rest of the team stood there helplessly, weeping and praying.

We were grief-stricken and shocked. Then, a spirit of determination triumphed. The work would not be stopped, not even by death and tragedy. 'God buries His workers, but His work carries on.'

However, some had another reaction. At home, some people began to make negative judgements. 'There must be sin in the team. Stop the work, stop the ministry, stop the whole operation.' I was amazed. If there was sin in the camp, God would not have needed to kill two fine men to let me know. Those pointing fingers of accusation were like Job's comforters, who tried to prove his miseries were a judgement from God. These people were home-bird Danites, sitting in their rocking chairs behind their ship shop tills. They handed out advice without cost to themselves.

To all such Danites we say that many are prepared to lay down their lives for Jesus in His work. Many a missionary has given his life for Africa. There are obvious dangers, such as Horst and Milton met, but those brothers were prepared to risk all. Others will not risk their money, let alone their lives, CfaN team members live with Jesus closely, day by day. We are on a real battlefield with Satan, who would like to destroy us. 'The blood of the martyrs is the seed of the church,' wrote St Tertullian 1,800 years ago, and his words have all history behind them as their proof today.

To die in the work of Christ may be the purpose of somebody's life. Christ is glorified whether people are won for Him by our deaths or by our lives. It is all the same. I offer this as my personal challenge to all who read this book—be a Zebulun or a Naphtali, and join the soldiers on the battlefield! The Lord is with us. Our Captain never lost a battle. It is time to give consideration to things other than material comforts. Begin to labour for that which does not perish.

To build God's eternal kingdom means that mortal hands do something that will be immortal. That which is of faith in God can never die. Levi left his tax collecting office once, the fisherman of Bethesda immediately followed Jesus, and these people are living in our affairs to this day. Now the call is to us. Jesus says, 'Follow Me!'

4

Gasping for the Gospel

If 10,000 people live around your church, four of them die every week, according to statistics. It is hardly satisfactory, then, if only one is saved every month, or even every week.

The need of the gospel is so blatant that anything I could say would be simply emphasising the obvious. Yet I see that the Devil has tricks to hide the obvious.

Satan first tried to stop the birth of the Saviour. He arranged the murder of Abel and launched hell's missiles at all Christ's human ancestors, finally slaughtering the innocents in Bethlehem. Murder and genocide having failed, the only alternative left was to prevent the preaching of the gospel.

At first, the Devil used only persecution and false gospels, but now he has a considerable armoury. One type of weapon he uses is to give believers other priorities. He doesn't mind how hard we work for our church, as long as it keeps us out of the mischief the gospel can work on his evil kingdom. We can major in doctrine, in fellowship, in prosperity or in cultivating our own soul, in ways that bear no relation to preaching the gospel to every creature. Good activities that, nonetheless, crowd out the most urgent work.

We even can devise interpretations of the Scriptures themselves which let us off the hook and quiet our consciences about the lost. Prayer itself, while so vital, can be substituted for evangelism. But, as Suzette Hattingh says, *'Prayer without evangelism is an arrow shot nowhere!'* If we hold prayer rallies, they should be linked to some direct evangelistic effort, and should not merely be for any and all general requests.

The world's needs are vast enough for everyone to see, and it would take a book to describe them all. If anything can help the woes of the globe, the gospel ranks at the top of the list. To preach the gospel is to unbind, while to withhold the gospel is to bind. Not to preach the gospel means that we hide the medicine from the patient!

Some have given up hope. They have seen the limits of science, technology, medicine, politics and education. Cynically they turn to opiates to forget. Drugs, drink, anything—even religious mysticism. The idea that man has only man to help him is frightening. Evil grows two heads for every one that we cut off. This hydra-headed monster needs the dagger of the cross of Christ plunged into its heart.

Every sphere of life cries out for the gospel, like a fish gasping on the bank for water. Personally, socially, globally, religiously, the *only* hope for us is in the gospel.

The gospel is the only new force available

Isaiah wrote that 'the whole head is sick, and the whole heart is faint' (Is 1:5). Sometimes our bodies cure themselves, but very often medicines are needed. These medicines reinforce the body's natural healing powers. Sickness can overcome the body's defences, and outside help is then needed. *When it comes to salvation, though, there is no other source for man except the supernatural power of the gospel.* Our task is to put that remedy on the table. There is no argument against the gospel's wonderful power, just because there are some people who will not accept it. One can never force a cure on somebody by any means whatsoever, not even by threat, if the patient resolves not to take it. The person will just die.

The history of Israel proves that when the Jews were true to their central faith, they did well. When they handed over their hearts to others, to new religions, heathens and superpowers, disaster followed automatically. The spiritual life of the people of Israel was always the deciding factor.

To treat faith in God as a secondary matter, or as a controversial side issue, is fatal. We are what we believe. All activity is regulated by faith. If we don't realise that, then we know nothing about human nature. *God* is the only issue that finally counts. The urgency of the gospel is impossible to exaggerate!

Fire insurance?

Now I want to tell you about the greatest need. One can't preach the gospel as a mere social benefit. The gospel has to do with God, and God has to do with eternity. If you want to consider the benefits here and now, they are obvious. To begin with, nothing adds up without God. Life is meaningless, as many atheists insist today. Only unbelievers feel so cynical.

Most of us, however, realise that God confronts us with the eternal ages. Our destiny is bound up in the gospel. 'Are you saved or lost?'—that is the question of all questions.

The declaration of the gospel is *'Jesus saves'*. He saves from wrath, judgement, hell, bondage, the Devil and darkness. He saves us from dying in our sins. I know some have scorned the gospel as 'fire insurance'. Well, what is

wrong with fire insurance, anyway? It is a crazy house-
holder who is not insured. We know, though, that salvation is much more. And who else offers such insurance but
Jesus?

Why humanity suffers

We all live and move and have our being in God. But
when we draw further and further away from Him, we
perish. We lose more and more of the reality of life. One
question regularly pondered is why God allows so much
suffering in the world. God 'allows suffering'? You might
just as well go and ask the government's Minister of
Transport why he allows accidents on the roads. The
minister would take exception to your accusation and
point to the book of traffic laws. 'Every time a law is
broken, an accident and suffering might occur,' he would
reply.

People suffer chiefly for one reason—they are ignoring
God's book, the Bible, and then everything goes wrong.
Our Creator knows how He made us, and consequently
says, 'Thou shalt not....' This 'thou shalt not' is not said
to spoil our fun, but because God knows that our psyche
cannot handle sin and actually is crushed by misdeeds. It
is always wise to read the instruction manual before using
a new appliance. People are worried about breaking a tape
recorder or a washing machine, but don't seem to mind
destroying their own spirits and souls with the poisons of
sin. The need to preach the gospel is desperate.

The meaning of the cross

Is the gospel a call to discipleship? People debate the
issue. One matter is sure—Jesus asks no one to take up
their cross until they have found salvation and strength at
His cross. We are not saved by denying ourselves and
carrying our own cross. We are saved by the redeeming
power of the atoning death of Jesus Christ, like the thief

who turned to the Lord while dying on the cross next to Him. We hope many will become disciples and take up their crosses, of course, but first they must kneel at His cross.

That cross of Jesus consists of two beams, one vertical and one horizontal. Those crossed timbers are twin symbols of human misery and God's salvation. The horizontal beam is like a dash, the very sign used for minus. That is the human story. We were born with a minus, a deficit, a void. Something is missing, but people are at a complete loss to know what it is. They talk about their search for truth, but they don't even know what they mean by truth. They are like Pontius Pilate who, standing before Jesus, nearly fell over *the* truth asking, 'What is truth?' That is man's minus outlook for you.

Jesus came, though. Outside Jerusalem, on a low hill, a vertical timber was raised which crossed through our minus sign. Jesus hung there on that upright, and He thus turned our minus into a plus. The Romans thought the cross was just an instrument of execution, but it was God's plus sign for minus-minded mankind.

Indeed, give the cross a second look, and it is even more than a plus—it is a multiplication sign. 'I am come that they might have life, *and that they might have it more abundantly*' (Jn 10:10, italics mine). The apostle Peter could write, 'Grace unto you, and peace, be multiplied' (1 Pet 1:2). Abundance is at the very heart of the gospel.

That is why we must preach this glorious gospel. Think of the many reversals the Saviour causes. Jesus Christ turns loss into gain, ciphers into numbers, negatives into positives, night into light, hate into love, bondage into freedom, failure into success, sickness into health, weakness into strength, evil into righteousness and more—so much more. What a gospel! Praise be to God. Nothing in all human knowledge can compete with that dazzling splendour. It is the greatest work on earth to preach the good news, and the need for the gospel is the greatest need in the world.

In a British city where I preached, someone told me that contractors had built a mosque and, as is customary, returned six months later to correct any fault which had developed. One door was sticking, and they sent a workman to rectify the problem. But the Muslim leader refused the repair, explaining that if the door was like that, it was the will of Allah and must remain as it was.

Jesus leaves nothing sticking and wrong. If it needs changing, He can change it, and He will. His will is never that which is faulty. The purpose of the gospel is to change a whole world which is wrong. Hallelujah!

The prodigal planet

If the subject of eternal life does not show the urgency of proclaiming the gospel to every creature, I cannot think of anything else that does more. True, other faiths are out there. But anyone who surveys them will know they are totally empty of any gospel promise. The mind cults of the East would offer only transient benefits, even if they did work. But the gospel does not have merely mental poise in view. The efforts the cults insist must be made to achieve harmony with nature are not worth while.

Jesus did not come to give us religious feelings or to suggest to us a system of mind power. He came to save us, not to explain how our 'inner resources' can be tapped to save ourselves. Jesus was not a teacher of TM, or quietism, or Stoicism. He was and is, first and foremost, a Saviour.

As for other religions, which of them offers eternal life *now?* Some only promise the end of existence. 'Karma' teachings see life as such a misery that obliteration is the only way out! Then there is the Paradise promise, which consists of endless sensual pleasure. That sounds more like hell than heaven to me.

The supreme wonder of the gospel is its present realisation of *life;* life of such quality that it cannot fade for eternity. 'Jesus said unto her, "I am the resurrection, and the life: he that believeth in me, though he were dead, yet shall he live: And whosoever liveth and believeth in me shall never die. Believest thou this?" ' (Jn 11:25–26).

That is the highest gospel possible! It is logically impossible to better it, and that life is available for us now. Urgent? The world gasps for the gospel like a fish out of water. Eternal life is the key gift, and that is the number one message, as well as the number one reason, for preaching the gospel.

The present world desperately needs the gospel! Why did God make the world? It was for good, for He is love. He filled it with pleasure that no man could exhaust, even if he lived for ever. Every conceivable taste and delight, for every sense we possess, came from the loving heart of God for His children.

When we go God's way, it is all ours. When we resist Him, we resist His own concern for us. We spoil His plans to bless us, and happiness is destroyed. We have reached the stage today where we are brilliant at destruction, from the ruin of graffiti upon walls to the threat of the obliteration of the entire environment. We war, we hate, we trample on the fair earth and foul all that He gives us.

Most of this destruction comes from sheer evil, or else from selfish greed. More basically, though, it comes from our turning away from God. Most of man's ills are man-made. The gospel reverses these fatal processes. It brings us back to do His will, and His will is always for the good of us all. God loves His prodigal planet, and if we return we shall enjoy the welcome of the Father and 'begin to be merry'.

I have seen it happen

God is sweeping some parts of the world with the gospel. The outcome is salvation: sins forgiven, racial harmony, crime wiped out, stolen property returned by the truck-load, marriages restored, families reunited, evil men

turned to saints, death-dealing addictions cured and miracles of healing. The gospel is the most elevating force on
earth. It has not come to level us all to the lowest common
denominator, but to create new creatures, and to give to
all the dignity of the sons of God! Men who once were
savages are reclaimed and walk as princes. What a reason
to preach the gospel! Could anything be more thrilling,
adventurous and worth while? What else is worth life's
effort?

The salvation of this world? Well, Jesus did not think it
a waste of time to go out of His way to heal the sick and
feed the feckless multitudes. He invited persecution for
healing a man with a withered arm, and from that
moment on He walked with a price on His head. That
man mattered to Jesus, and his arm had to be restored, no
matter what (Mt 12:10).

People who believe in the gospel also believe in people
and in caring for their physical needs. The less we believe
in God, the less we value mankind. Atheism bred Adolf
Hitler and Joseph Stalin, and put millions out of existence
as if they were not more than figures in chalk on a child's
blackboard. Preaching the gospel is part of God's plan to
put us, as it were, back in Eden.

Nonetheless, suppose the impossible—that science and
politics could put us back in the Garden of Eden. Would
that last long, and wouldn't our restlessness reduce it once
again to ruin? There is one reason we desire Eden, though
many do not realise it—mankind wants those conditions
again in which they heard the voice of God in the Garden.
No mansion would suit a bride without her bridegroom!
No earthly paradise would suit us without the love and
words of God.

Some churchmen say that 'man is a social animal', as if
the herd instinct was all that could be mentioned about
that marvellous creation called man. We are more than a
herd—we are each made for God, and nothing else but a
relationship with Him will ever content us.

Sometimes, when inspired music touches us, we get a

sense of infinity. Music only points to it, though. The music echoes a faraway greatness that it cannot fulfil. That infinity is God Himself, and what music only suggests is given to us when we receive salvation through Jesus Christ and begin to worship Him.

God is our natural habitat. Until we find Him, as we do when we obey the gospel, we are caged. Men everywhere are beating themselves against the bars of their own materialism and unbelief. Their very money becomes their prison. Deep calls to deep, and height to height, within our souls. Our art, our poetry, our works of beauty are the expressions of imprisoned creatures who remember the glories of the free air and the mountains. While good in themselves, these expressions remain mere reflections of reality until a soul comes into salvation. Jesus is the reality behind all that we see or do, and the gospel releases us from bondage, allowing us to come into our true element!

Somebody said that 'Christians are happy in their way'. In their way? In what sort of way are unbelievers happy? In no sort of way, I think. Christians are happy in God's way, the originally intended way. The God scene is the only scene. Outside are the wastes of the wilderness and the horizons where dawn never breaks, where the godless will never be happy in any way. Unbelievers will have to extract what drink they can from the dry ground of resentment, doubt and hatred. But the Spirit and the Bride say, 'Come...and drink from the fountain of life freely'(Rev 22:17). A way of life is preached in the gospel that leads more and more unto the perfect day. That is another reason for the need to preach the gospel. Could there be a greater urgency?

PART TWO

The Gospel

5

God's New Elishas

The Great Commission to each generation

Christ's Great Commission is not a scrap of paper, blown
to our feet from centuries ago. It is Jesus, standing in the
midst of His church for ever, saying, 'Go ye...for I am
with you.'

Suppose He said it to you personally—would you take
more notice of it? Just imagine that you had a vision of the
Lord in your church, like John had on Patmos. Suppose
that Jesus spoke to everybody, saying, 'Go ye into all the
world and preach the gospel to every creature and signs
shall follow them that believe.' What would you do?
Would you carry on just the same as usual? Or would you
press on more urgently to witness for Christ?

If anyone wonders whether the Great Commission is
'relevant' today, they may as well ask if ploughing and
harvesting are relevant—or if getting out of bed is! 'Relevant' is not the word. The task is urgent. It is supposed to
be our existence. A Christian is a witness. The name
'Christian' arose because it easily identified believers—
they were the people who always talked about Christ. The

Christian's business is not busy-ness but witness. Witness-ing is the commerce of the people of the kingdom of God.

The written commands of Christ in Scripture are just as immediate as if He spoke to us personally in a vision. The Great Commission is 'our baby', and our work in this task is not optional. The Lord does not ask, 'Would you mind helping Me? I would like to invite you.' He says: 'Ye have not chosen me, but I have chosen you, and ordained you, that ye should go and bring forth fruit, and that your fruit should remain' (Jn 15:16).

In this verse, He was not talking about the election to salvation, but rather of the election to service. We do not serve at our discretion. The Great Commission is a draft 'call-up', not a suggestion for our consideration.

In fact, Christ's command is much more than that. Jesus turns us into witnesses. He changes our nature by His Spirit within us. He did not tell us, 'Witness!' He said, 'Be witnesses!' It was a creative word. God said, 'Let there be light,' and light broke in upon us. He chose us and then made us light-bearers.

'For we are his workmanship, created in Christ Jesus unto good works' (Eph 2:10). These good works are to 'shew the exceeding riches of his grace' (v 7). If we do not show the world the riches of His grace, it would be foreign to our new nature in Christ. What the Holy Spirit has planted within us is the Spirit of witness. But we can become slack and let the light within us die down through neglect. Fruitless branches are purged.

Now we have a wonderful guarantee. When we go as He says, He goes with us. Evangelism and witness are the way to be sure He is with you. Suppose we do not com-ply—is He still with us? Well, one thing is sure. The anointing of the Spirit only comes with obedience. The anointing and the Great Commission go together. This is what I want to inspire you to realise now.

Transferred mandate

Here is a word from the Lord for us today. His voice came to me from a corner of the Bible not always noticed (1 Kings 19:15–16):

> And the Lord said unto [Elijah], 'Go, return on thy way to the wilderness of Damascus...anoint Hazael to be king over Syria: And Jehu the son of Nimshi shalt thou anoint to be king over Israel: and Elisha the son of Shaphat of Abelmeholah shalt thou anoint to be prophet in thy room.'

Three men had to be anointed—Hazael, Jehu and Elisha. That is straightforward, and not so very remarkable. However, what actually happened is another matter. This great prophet Elijah failed to carry out two-thirds of God's command. He never anointed Hazael or Jehu. In fact, we don't read that he actually anointed Elisha, either, but Elijah did go and find him. When his mantle rested on Elisha, Elisha received a 'double portion' of Elijah's spirit. That is, the same Spirit that had anointed Elijah then anointed Elisha to carry out the same commission. Later, it was Elisha who anointed Hazael and Jehu.

So now we see a very important fact—Elijah's commission, with Elijah's power, transmitted itself to Elisha. A dual transfer took place from the prophet who was leaving to the prophet who was staying. Elisha received Elijah's enduement, but that anointing was to fulfil Elijah's task. God's commission and authority remained when Elijah left, falling upon Elisha. The mandate was transferable.

That is a divine principle. God's call and His power are transferable. The Great Commission, and the promises that go with it, made the disciples what they eventually would become. The same commission and the same promises were passed on to us, in order that we could do and be what the first disciples did and were. We are the heirs of the apostles.

Now the commission of Christ to us is far more important than Elijah's commission, and the promised anointing
is even greater. Read it again:

> Go ye therefore, and teach all nations, baptizing them in the
> name of the Father, and of the Son, and of the Holy Ghost:
> Teaching them to observe all things whatsoever I have com-
> manded you: and lo, I am with you alway, even unto the end
> of the world. Amen (Mt 28:19–20).

Note that it reads, 'Even unto the end of the world.' The
New International Version translates it, 'To the very end
of the age'—that entails now, tomorrow and beyond. This
means that, if Jesus did appear and speak to us today, He
would say the same thing. He has never changed.

People want to know what the Lord is saying to the
church. He no doubt has many things to say, just as He
did in the 'Letters of Jesus' in the Book of Revelation. But
if we are not busy doing what He already has told us to do,
He will only have one thing to say—'Get on with it!' So:
'Hear what the Spirit says to the churches.' Why wait for
another letter when you have not opened the first one yet?
Jesus has no further word for us until His standing orders
are carried out.

Many are waiting for God to speak, but only if He says
what they want Him to say. They wait and wait for God to
give them a new direction. But how do they know He has a
new direction for them? Or that He has a great new
revelation? Or that He will give them radical instructions?
The word from God I have is that He wants the old
direction—a witnessing church, with evangelism in and
through the churches (1 Jn 2:7). Let me spell this out: until
this major command is put into effect, everything else is
irrelevant.

On my part, I believe we should have a humble attitude and indeed pray that the mantle of earlier men and
women of God will rest upon us. There would be no
church but for their power in revival. Many of them were
true Elijahs. (I have something very thrilling to say about

that in a moment.) They took up the Great Commission and became God's brightest luminaries.

John had the mind of Jesus when he wrote, 'I write no new commandment unto you, but an old commandment which ye had from the beginning' (1 Jn 2:7). Jesus doesn't keep on issuing fresh legislation, like governments do today. What He once said, He has said *once;* once and for all. His word is still His will.

Whatever 'new thing' He says is in His word already. There are no hidden secrets for superior saints. His instructions simply say, 'Go!'

A motorist waiting at some traffic lights was inattentive as the light changed from red to green. An irritable driver behind him jumped out of his vehicle and said to him, 'That light says "go"! Are you waiting for the Minister of Transport's personal confirmation?' We have a green light from God. Let's go!

No hand-me-downs

There is something else I must tell you. We do not read that Elijah ever instructed Elisha to anoint Hazael and Jehu. Although he inherited Elijah's commission, God must have told Elisha personally. Even though we are linked up with generations of God's people before us, the Great Commission is transferred to us by the Lord Himself. Jesus continues to point to the original Great Commission. God always operates with originals. His mandate is direct, and not by tradition.

'How shall they preach, except they be sent?' (Rom 10:15). The Spirit says the same thing. He directs us. The Holy Spirit is the Spirit of witness. Witness is His purpose. The Great Commission is linked to the Holy Spirit. When Christ baptises us into the Spirit, He puts into our hands His instructions to take the gospel to the whole world.

Everything comes from the Master Himself—not in a general way, but in an individual way. Jesus alone is the Baptiser, and we please Him when we engage in the work

He sends us to do. Baptising multitudes in water is a strenuous job, but Christ has reserved for Himself the task of baptising us, as individuals, into the Holy Spirit. We don't go to men for their power. Everyone can get his own Holy Spirit baptism direct from the Lord. We are not called by the will of men, but rather by the will of God. Paul begins seven of his epistles with just that emphasis. Along with the call comes the power, the enablement. I can put my hands on men and women, praying in my heart that God will bless and use them. We may lay our hands on people to receive the baptism into the Holy Spirit, just as the apostles did. But Jesus alone baptises. Jesus said, 'I [note, "I"] have...ordained you' (Jn 15:16).

If the anointing had to be transferred from hand to hand since the Day of Pentecost, or if it could only be passed on by the early apostles, the church would have become one of history's lost causes long ago. We can have fresh oil from the Lord. The wise virgins did not share their oil (Mt 25:8–9). Each of us must have our own oil, direct from Jesus.

The package deal

The Great Commission to the disciples is transferred to each one of us individually today, and it comes with the individual anointing of the Holy Spirit. The command and the power are one package deal. Jesus told His disciples to tarry in Jerusalem until they were endued with power, so that then they would be witnesses in all the world. Separate the commission from the enabling, and you then have either power without purpose or purpose without power. Power tools come with the job. Go with bare hands and you will make little progress.

One with the apostles

I have looked forward to writing the next passage. I began by explaining what Elijah had placed upon Elisha. The same endowment came upon John the Baptist. We read that he came in the Spirit and power of Elijah (Lk 1:17). What made Elijah a great prophet, and what made Elisha a great prophet, was what made John the Baptist a great prophet, too. Jesus called John 'the greatest born of woman'.

That was not the last of the matter. The same Spirit who was upon Elijah made the apostles what they were. Still, it didn't all end there. The Spirit rested upon the martyrs and the confessors, too, as well as on those who followed. Has He now vanished? No—the thrilling truth is that the Spirit which made them one with Elijah makes us one with them all. He is still here—we can include ourselves in His company. The Spirit of Elijah and Elisha, of John, of the apostles and of the early church has never left. He has been among men ever since, generation after generation. That same Spirit is our inheritance. We were born to belong to His company.

We are in God's revival team, right alongside Whitefield and Wesley, Finney and Evans, Wigglesworth, Price and Jeffreys. We share the platform, hand in hand with all God's anointed ones. We—yes, we—come in the Holy Spirit, the Spirit and the power of Elijah. What belonged to the great men of God is ours, and what is ours was once theirs. The Holy Spirit is the Spirit of the prophets, poured out upon all flesh today.

These believers were all Elijahs, and we now are all their Elishas. What they did, we shall do. Jesus said, 'Other men laboured, and ye are entered into their labours.' We identify with them all. They brought the flame of Pentecost to us right from the Upper Room in Jerusalem, and now we carry it further. What inspired them inspires us—the same gospel, the same Book, the same love, the same Christ of Calvary and the same Holy Spirit.

The men of the historic revivals have departed. All have gone—except for the chief figure, Jesus Christ. The One who met Saul on the Damascus Road and Peter in

Galilee—He is here! He is with us! He is still baptising into the Holy Spirit.

With the same anointing will often come the same persecutions. The Great Commission, the anointing and the opposition go together. As always, the followers of Jesus will be defamed and mocked by the wise of this world. They will consider you, a believer, to be out of touch if you do not follow them in their unbeliefs and in the so-called science of biblical rationalism. These who expound this rationalism begin with a non-miraculous creed, and then take the scissors to Scripture to make it fit.

If we share Christ's work, we share in His suffering. But 'if we suffer we shall also reign with Him'. If we are derided for our faith in God, we shall reign by our faith in God. When people say the same things about you as they said about God's people in the past, rejoice that you are identified with them. Whoever treats you as the New Testament people were treated proves that you belong to that glorious New Testament company. When you carry out the same commission they did, with the same authority, you will also have the same enemies. Whenever the Devil treats you as his foe, rejoice! He is paying you the best compliment possible. He is ranking you with those he hated in the past, the beloved servants of the Most High God.

David Livingstone's prophecy

In 1986 we had one of our greatest gospel crusades ever in Blantyre, Malawi, in East Africa. The attendance climbed to a peak of 150,000 per service. Blantyre is named after the town in Scotland where the great missionary David Livingstone was born. Livingstone had planted a Christian mission in the area and had founded a city that now has 300,000 inhabitants, making it the largest city in Malawi today.

Let me quote from his diary:

We are like voices crying in the wilderness; we prepare the way for a glorious future. Future missionaries will be rewarded with conversions for every sermon. We are their pioneers and helpers.

Let them not forget the watchmen of the night—us, who worked when all was gloom, and no evidence of success in the way of conversion cheered our paths. They will doubtlessly have more light than we; but we can serve our Master earnestly and proclaim the gospel as they will do.

Livingstone died in 1873. So we were there more than 100 years later. What about Livingstone's prophetic word? Was it merely wishful thinking? I rejoice to tell you what we saw. The seed sown so long ago is now blooming into harvest. The people of Malawi heard about the same God as Livingstone's, the same Saviour as Paul's, the same gospel as Peter's. We were there sixteen days, and tens of thousands responded to Livingstone's message as we preached it for him and for Jesus. It reverberated throughout the whole country. The Holy Spirit spoke to my heart and said, 'You are walking on the tears of former generations.'

Suddenly, I saw it all. We are linked up in God in a movement that consists of His earlier workers, too, and so are one with them all. We belong to their team, to their mission. We were reaping with joy where they had sown in tears before us. We did not have this harvest because we were superior to those previous men and women, but only because the harvest season had arrived. Both those who have sown and those who reap will receive the reward, according to the word of the Lord of the harvest, Jesus. He said, 'He that reapeth receiveth wages, and gathereth fruit unto life eternal: that both he that soweth and he that reapeth may rejoice together...I sent you to reap that whereon ye bestowed no labour: other men laboured, and ye are entered into their labours' (Jn 4:36–38).

This is harvest time—believe it! The world's multitudes have multiplied. The opportunity is vast, exciting. And we, you, all of us, are the privileged ones chosen to do the reaping. Knowing that so much was done already, long before we ever arrived on the scene, should keep us humble in times of success. We are trusted not to fail the sowers. We owe it to them to put in the sickle, or better still, to use a combine harvester. The Elijahs, the Pauls, the Justin Martyrs, the Livingstones—all relied on us for the future. They expected us to take advantage of all their labours. We cannot be proud—only privileged.

A remarkable meeting

In 1961, at twenty-one years old, I completed my Bible College studies in the United Kingdom. I could then go home to northern Germany. The route took me via London. My train was not due to leave until the evening, so I had time to do some sightseeing. I just walked as my feet took me, without a plan, and somehow wandered south of the River Thames into the pleasant avenues of Clapham.

Then, at a certain corner, behind a high wooden fence, I saw a name on a panel—'George Jeffreys'. I had just read a book by this evangelist, and could hardly imagine that I had chanced upon the very house where that same man might be. George Jeffreys came out of the Welsh revival and, with his brother Stephen and other members of the Jeffreys family, had introduced the pentecostal message publicly to the people of Britain. His work shook cities, and tens of thousands witnessed mighty miracles. Eagerly I ventured through the gate and up the path, ringing the doorbell. A lady appeared and I asked, 'Is this the George Jeffreys whom God used so mightily?' She affirmed it was so, to my great delight. I asked, hopefully, 'Could I please see Mr Jeffreys?' The reply was firm. 'No, that is not possible.'

But then that deep, musical Welsh voice, that is said to have held thousands spellbound with its authority, spoke from inside. 'Let him come in.' Thrilled, I entered, and there he was. He was seventy-two, but looked to me like a man of ninety.

'What do you want?' were his words to me. I introduced myself, and then we talked about the work of God. Suddenly, the great man fell on his knees, pulling me down with him, and started to bless me. The power of the Holy Spirit entered that room. The anointing began to flow, and, like Aaron's. oil, seemed to run over my head and 'down to the skirts of my robes', so to speak.

I left that house dazed. Four weeks later, like Elijah, George Jeffreys had been translated to glory. I had been led to see him just before he died. But I knew that I had picked up something from this former Holy Ghost, firebrand evangelist. The Lord, I am sure, had arranged that meeting. How else would it have been possible for me to stumble upon this one house in a city of ten million people, when George Jeffreys was not even on my mind? Whatever this experience did for me, one thing I can claim. Seeing this man of God made me understand that we build on the people who went before us. The city of God is built on the foundations of the apostles. We can liken it to a relay race. One man runs with a baton, another man grabs it and runs, and then another and another. They all share in the race and in the victory. If one drops the baton, or even runs a little badly, the efforts of all the rest are spoiled, and the whole team loses.

We read about the 'cloud of witnesses'. They stand looking over the battlements of glory, cheering us on. We are running for them. We must do a little more than they did, not a little less. It is the last lap before Jesus comes. We cannot rest on *their* laurels. The great finish line is in sight. Do you see, now, what the following Scripture means? 'And the gospel of the kingdom shall be preached in all the world for a witness unto all nations; and then shall the end come' (Mt 24:14).

What is the theme of the hour, or the slogan for today? Not our theme, mind you, but God's theme. It is 'evangelism by fire', which is, in and of itself, an initiative for revival. It is evangelism by the gifts, the power and the manifestation of the Holy Spirit.

I want to ask you a question. Do you find it hard to win souls for Jesus, and so have stopped trying? Well, shouldn't that problem be first on your agenda? What is first on your church agenda, or on your conference agenda, or on your personal agenda? Is it a resolution that nothing can be done because times are difficult? God has a way for you, by His Spirit.

Dr David H C Read writes about a young minister in a tough area of New York, who poured out his woes about the difficulties to a local policeman. The officer tried to cheer him up, saying, 'The fact is, Reverend, this is not the kind of district for a Christian church.' These words woke him up. What else, he thought, is a Christian church supposed to be doing, if not operating where the need is greatest?

Doubters like to be clever. They analyse the situation and point out the impossibilities with high-flown language. They 'prove' that nothing can be done, using words like pluralism, hedonism, insularism and narcissism, showing, with high-sounding terms, that the situation is hopeless. You would think that God hasn't taken all of this into consideration.

The doubters are wrong. This is God's reaping time. Something can be done—God has prepared for everything, not by might, nor by power, but by His Spirit. This is what we are to rely upon—not television, radio, money or education, but the miracle power of Jesus.

We have only one generation to reach this generation. The original gospel mandate is impossible without the original power. The perfect strategy of God is complete. He included you in it, and He included me in it. We are woven into and enmeshed in His plans, plans that cannot fail. If we know that, then we can do it...weather it...finish it...no matter what.

6

The Matchless Message

Don't argue—shine! You can't conquer darkness by arguing with it. Just switch the light on. The gospel is power, power for light. Preach it. Then you are plugged in, and the light comes.

God's power lines draw current from Calvary, from the Resurrection and from the throne, for 'the gospel...is the power of God,' wrote the apostle Paul (Rom 1:16). He knew. He had proved it. The world then could not have been worse; cruel, corrupt and cynical. Yet the gospel changed it. The gospel can do it again.

How to let the power gospel loose on the world

One preacher told me he wanted a transformer to reduce the emotional appeal of the gospel, to turn the message from high voltage to low voltage. But converting sinners requires full gospel power. Preach to convict and convert. Your job is not to entertain, not to make people smile and go home feeling cosy. Salvation is not soothing syrup. Save souls, don't stroke them! Smiling happiness will follow.

Read about Philip the evangelist meeting the Ethiopian official. The Ethiopian was the queen's financial chief, a man of business, with no time for small talk. Philip didn't bother to ask what his needs were in order to start counselling him for hours. Philip knew the man's needs. The eunuch needed Christ. Salvation is everyone's need. Philip got down to essentials. He 'preached unto him Jesus' (Acts 8:35).

Jesus is the beginning and the end of every gospel sermon, the Alpha and the Omega of all witness. We are not doctrine mongers. We are not religion pushers. We are not enthusiasts. We are witnesses to Christ. He is the be-all-and-the-end-all of the message.

What did Jesus preach? He talked about Himself. On the Emmaus road, walking with Cleopas and a friend, He explained to them, going throughout the Scriptures, the 'things concerning himself' (Lk 24:27).

All His teaching goes back to Himself. Take one instance, for example. After He had left Nazareth and begun His wonderful ministry, He returned one day and went into the synagogue. For twenty years He had attended that very synagogue every week. The custom was to allow men who were known to read the Scriptures, and perhaps comment on them afterwards. Naturally, when He was present at the synagogue again, He was invited to do this.

The gospel message is in the Old Testament—in fact, the Old Testament is full of the gospel. So Jesus read from Isaiah 61:1–2:

> The Spirit of the Lord is upon me; because he hath anointed me to preach the gospel to the poor; he hath sent me to heal the broken-hearted; to preach deliverance to the captives; and the recovering of sight to the blind; to set at liberty them that are bruised; to preach the acceptable year of the Lord.

Nobody in the synagogue thought much of that. They knew the words by heart, and those words had been read for 800 years. The scroll of the Scripture was handed back, the synagogue leader took it with great reverence, kissed it, and put it away—to be forgotten until next week. But, suddenly, that scroll seemed to become a stick of dynamite. The word in the lips of Jesus produced effects all right. It awakened the drowsy congregation. He showed them that the word was about Himself. There are seven distinct statements in that verse and they all apply to Him, as well as to the present. 'Today,' He said, 'this scripture is fulfilled in your ears.' He declared Himself to be the Anointed One, the Christ, the One to perform all those promised exploits.

The acceptable year

The first six statements can be summed up in the last one: 'To proclaim the acceptable year of the Lord.' That 'acceptable year', is actually the Jubilee year. The word 'Jubilee' is a Hebrew word. It is God's idea or thought. The Jubilee was instituted to give everybody a holiday for a year, to set free all bondservants and to cancel all debts.

Unfortunately, it appears that the Jubilee trumpet was never blown. The nation never had a sabbatical year, and that was a failure which God held against them. The Lord would have been delighted with such gladness—God's style is to promote happiness. Even though the country did not celebrate the Jubilee year, God meant to have it. His Jubilee would be in a far greater fashion, as we shall see. But the Jubilee of Moses is described in Leviticus 25:8–17:

> Then shalt thou cause the trumpet of the jubilee to sound on the tenth day of the seventh month—and ye shall hallow the fiftieth year, and proclaim liberty throughout all the land unto all the inhabitants thereof: it shall be a jubilee unto you.... Ye shall not therefore oppress one another...for I am the Lord your God.

Proclaim liberty! Do not preach for effects, for pulpit display, or to charm, excite, or scare folk. Do not preach to calm people down. You can preach for all kinds of effects, but Jesus simply announced liberty. He proclaimed, that day in the synagogue, that the Jubilee had begun. He showed them what a true Jubilee would be—deliverance. A Jubilee, not merely for Israel, but for the whole world. A Jubilee for people like the foreigners He mentioned—Naaman, the Syrian leper and the widow of Zarephath.

The synagogue congregation marvelled at this new teaching. They were lost in this unfamiliar landscape of Christ's prospects for the entire world. The world He loved was too big for them. Their fears were roused. Then, murderous passions were ignited, feelings that were never too far below the surface in those days. Jesus' sermon certainly produced a response—the members of the congregation attempted to throw Him over a precipice!

Yet, His message was wonderful—freedom, deliverance, healing and no debts. But, whatever the reaction, Jesus preached His gospel. So must we.

Debt in those days was tragic. Fathers and their families became slaves and could never get free. Only the Jubilee could release them. The debtors could go home. If anyone did not return, it was his own fault. The law said, 'Go!' Any slave after the Jubilee was a slave by his own choice.

Jesus Christ has proclaimed the Jubilee for the whole human race. All that Israel knew about Jubilees now became only a poor image of the real Jubilee of the kingdom of God. Lives set free, sins' debts wiped out, deliverance for body, spirit and soul. There are no sweating slaves in that kingdom. No fetters. Nobody Devil-driven. Hallelujah! What a Jubilee! Isaiah describes it:

> To give unto them beauty for ashes, the oil of joy for mourning, the garment of praise for the spirit of heaviness...They shall build the old wastes, they shall raise up the former desolations, and they shall repair the waste cities...eat the riches of the Gentiles.... Everlasting joy shall be unto them...no more termed Forsaken...salvation cometh...and they shall call them...the redeemed of the Lord (Is 61–62).

In Nazareth, the Lord turned these old scriptures into a royal proclamation of a new dispensation. He announced an amnesty for all prisoners of the Devil—'He led captivity captive'. 'Sin shall not have dominion over you,' states the Scriptures, and, 'When the fulness of the time was come, God sent forth his Son...to redeem them that were under the law' (Gal 4:4–5).

The Jubilee is now

This is 'the acceptable year of the Lord'. High technology has not made deliverance unnecessary. In every nation, the enslaved abound—slaves to every contemptible habit, slaves to fear, slaves to doubt, slaves to depression. The Devil never lets anyone out on parole. Everywhere people are failure-prone, sin-prone, morally defective, spiritually in chains. How ridiculous. Why? This is jubilee!

Preach it! People have forgotten it. Forgotten that Christ has been. This is not the pre-Christian era. We are not waiting for Christ to come and conquer. The war is over. Freedom is ours. Jesus opened the kingdom of liberty and blew the trumpet of emancipation when He cried on the Cross, 'It is finished!'

People who should know better are calling this the 'post-Christian' era, as if the work of Christ was only for a past age. That certainly is not true. Christ opened prison doors for ever, not just for a certain period in the past. The work of Jesus cannot be exhausted or undone. It is the greatest redemptive force at work on earth today. Never again can prison doors be bolted on human beings. When Jesus opens a door, no man can shut it. 'He whom the Son makes free is free indeed.' Why do millions languish in the Devil's concentration camp? Today is the day of amnesty. The Conquerer has crashed through the gates—relief has arrived.

The most famous escaper of all was Houdini, a show business notable. Police would lock him up in a cell and, as they walked away, he would follow them—already

loose within seconds. Except once. Half an hour went by
and Houdini was still fuming over the lock. Then a policeman came and simply pushed the door open. The door
had never been locked! Houdini was fooled trying to
unlock a door which was already unlocked.

Christ has gone right through the castle of Giant
Despair. He has the keys of death and hell, and He has
opened the gates. So why are millions sweating, trying
every trick to get out of their evil habits and bondages?
They join new cults or old heathen religions, hear new
theories, go to psychiatrists. But why? Jesus does set men
free. He does it all the time.

That's the gospel! You don't preach *about* it, or offer its
contents for discussion. The gospel is not a discussion
point. It is a proclamation of deliverance. Dialogue? The
gospel is not open to modification. It is mandatory, a royal
and divine edict. Some systems and theories of deliverance
are bondages in themselves, full of life-long duties and
demands. Only Jesus saves.

I remember a man who told me that he also was a
'spiritual counsellor'. However, he didn't believe that
Jesus Christ was the Son of God, nor that the Bible was
the word of God. I wondered, therefore, how this 'counsellor' counselled anybody. 'Do they come to you and then
go away with broken hearts?' I asked. 'Oh no,' he assured
me, 'I just calm them down.' I looked him in the eye and
said, 'Mister, a man on a sinking ship needs more than a
tranquilliser. Don't calm him down. He is going down
already. When Jesus comes to a man in a shipwreck, He
doesn't throw him a Valium tablet and say, "Perish in
peace." He reaches down His nail-scarred hand, grips
him, lifts him and says to him, "I live and you shall live
also." '

This is the gospel of Jesus Christ that must be
preached. Jesus is the Saviour of our world. This message
is life, peace and health for spirit, soul and body.

How the anointing breaks the yoke

Jesus said, 'The Spirit of the Lord is upon me because he
hath anointed me.' He is the 'anointed one' of this new
dispensation. That is exactly how the first gospel
preacher, the apostle Peter, understood it. He told his
audience (the first Europeans to hear the gospel), that
'God anointed Jesus of Nazareth with the Holy Ghost and
with power: who went about doing good, and healing all
that were oppressed of the devil; for God was with him'
(Acts 10:38).

The expression 'the Anointed' is the same as 'Christ'.
To say, 'Jesus Christ,' is to say, 'Jesus the Anointed One.'

Now, was He anointed only while He was here on
earth? If so, we should not call Him 'Christ' any more. But
if He is the same, then He is the 'Anointed One' still
today. That is what He is, exactly as is said of Him in
Hebrews 13:8: 'Jesus Christ the same yesterday, and
today, and for ever.' Not 'Jesus' alone, but 'Jesus Christ,
the Anointed One'.

This is also what we read in John 1:33: 'Upon whom
thou shalt see the Spirit descending, *and remaining* on him,
the same is he which baptizeth with the Holy Ghost'
(italics mine). The Holy Spirit *remains* with Him, which is
why He still baptises in the Holy Spirit. This was an
important point in Peter's first sermon in Acts 2:36: 'God
hath made that same Jesus, whom ye have crucified, both
Lord and Christ.' Peter's preaching was after Jesus' death
and ascension. Following that instance in Acts, right
throughout the New Testament to Revelation, Jesus is
called 'Christ' in every major book. Ten times in the first
ten verses of 1 Corinthians, the emphasis is on 'the Lord
Jesus Christ'. In chapter 2:2: 'For I determined not to
know any thing among you, save Jesus Christ, and him
crucified.' Just as He is still our crucified Lord, He is still
our Anointed One.

If Jesus no longer delivers, no longer heals, no longer
saves, no longer casts out demons, no longer baptises into
the Spirit, then we have a Jesus who is no longer 'Christ',

for that is the very meaning of the title and name 'Jesus Christ'. He is 'the same yesterday, and today, and for ever', and if He has changed, then He has forgotten to tell us. But we have no evidence for any such thing.

Apart from the exact meaning of His title, what Jesus was and is also must be taken into proper account. We will take up that issue in the next chapter.

7

Jesus—Robed or Stripped?

When people go to church, they want Jesus. Not politics. Not sentimentalism. Not the man of Galilee as a distant, ideal figure. They don't want a phantom, a myth. If they have read the Bible, they want to meet that same Jesus in all His glorious vitality. Who wouldn't? Preach that Jesus, and the Holy Spirit is bound to reveal Him. He will step into the midst of the crowd, just as He promised.

In our crusades, both in Africa and elsewhere, we have seen the Anointed Jesus at work, doing all He was anointed to do. We have seen Him sweeping into the world today with the winds of heaven. He has drawn together multitudes so great that they are only counted by the acre. Thousands are being healed, saved and baptised into the Holy Spirit at one time.

How to know which Christ to preach

When I see miracles happening, miracles of healing, miracles of changed lives, miracles of cleansed sinners, I know who is at work. It is the Anointed One. These wonders are

His fingerprint, His hallmark. *This* Christ is the Christ to preach: the yesterday-today-for-ever Christ. Every time we use His name, Jesus Christ, it is a declaration that He is anointed to deliver. When there are wonders, that's how we know He is the real Christ. Miracles are His identity card, His genetic coding.

How was it that John knew it was Jesus, one misty morning in the partial darkness? Jesus was on shore, way up on the beach, while John sat in a boat 100 yards from the water's edge. Yet, he recognised Jesus (Jn 21:7). How? He recognised what Jesus did.

Jesus called to the disciples, telling them to cast their nets, just as He had told them when He first met them. They had a heavy catch of great fish again, just as they had had three years before. 'It must be the same Jesus,' John concluded, and he cried out, 'It is the Lord!' His actions revealed His personage. But how can people know He is the same Jesus if He doesn't do the same things? How can they know Him if He is not even preached as the same One—the One who worked wonders and transformed human lives? How can anyone dare to call Him Christ and say that He doesn't work miracles? His anointing guaranteed that He would be a miracle worker.

Jesus is *Christ* Jesus, the Anointed Jesus. He is the One to preach. The following is an important statement: 'Jesus can only be what you preach Him to be.'

The Holy Spirit can only bless what you say about Jesus. The Spirit cannot bless what you *don't* say about Him. If 'this same Jesus', the very 'Jesus whom Paul preacheth', is preached now, the Spirit of God will confirm it. Preach a limited Jesus, and He cannot be Himself. He doesn't save unless you preach a Saviour. He doesn't heal unless you preach the Healer. How many are guilty of stripping our precious Lord? Men stripped Him once for His crucifixion; unbelief strips Him again of His power. He is no longer mighty to save and heal in many a church. Using Paul's expression, He is 'straightened' in our lives, which means 'hemmed in with no room to work' (2 Cor 6:12).

How to make the gospel news

A schoolboy once asked, 'How can you call something news which is 2,000 years old? Jesus is history, not news.' He made a mistake. Only dead people are history. Jesus is alive and active throughout the world. He is a world figure, and all world figures are news, especially this One.

The word 'gospel' comes from the Old English, 'god' (good) and 'spell' (message). It is a translation of *evangelion*, the Greek original. The gospel is not only what Jesus did, but what He does. Acts 1:1 states, 'I [wrote about] all that Jesus began both to do and teach.' He began to do it, and He is still doing it. He is making news today.

Two thousand years are nothing to Him. The sun is old, but active. The Bible is old, but powerful. If a telephone directory contains all the right numbers, I don't care how old it is. I take the Bible, and every time I dial, I get through to the throne of God. The gospel is God's word. One of the greatest minds of modern times was that of Immanuel Kant, the German philosopher. He said, 'The existence of the Bible is the greatest blessing which humanity ever experienced.' It is, if it is preached. But it is a major occupation of some men of the church to spend time merely trying to find out who wrote it and when, as if it mattered. Meanwhile, millions die of spiritual hunger and are lost for ever.

How to make the gospel happen

If the gospel is just left as an idea, 'the letter killeth'. But when it is preached under the power of the Holy Spirit, it generates power. Under proper conditions, following the right formula, a process begins; something takes place. If you take the truth of Jesus and preach it with the power of the Spirit, you are using God's formula. Such a formula produces results. When the Holy Spirit and gospel preaching come together, there is an explosion of power. Divine energy is released. Paul used the word *energemata*, which is 'out-working energy'. When such an explosion occurs, the gospel is then news.

When that heavenly force breaks upon us, there are highly unorthodox and interesting effects. There is revival. The graveyard atmosphere is gone. Meetings cease to be mere form and ritual. This power is not a blind force. It is Jesus at work again.

The stupifying fact about Christendom is that tens of millions struggle on as if Christ had never been. They talk about Him, but as the world's most conspicuous absentee. They act as if His first advent was entirely fruitless. People try on their own to be brave and to manage, but haven't managed yet. Mostly it is ignorance of the gospel and its power, which could be blamed on us, the church.

Yet all around are Christ's footprints. There is the church. Modern miracles. Bibles. Christian festivals. His sayings are part of our language. All that is best in civilisation, our morals and principles, are here because He came. Yet people drag themselves through life as if they haven't a clue. They creep in the shadows, afraid of the dawn. They talk of wanting a new religion, but have never tried the Christian faith. 'The word is nigh thee', but familiarity breeds contempt. The trouble is that they have built their nuclear power plants higher than the churches. The nuclear age is powerless.

There is vast demand for the real thing, however. Too many suppose that Christianity doesn't work any more. The church is a museum. The Bible may as well have been discovered in Tutankhamen's tomb—as if the word were only for ancient Israel! That is why we must preach the gospel in the power of the Spirit, with signs and wonders following. Then Jesus will step out of the Bible into modern life. Don't shut Him up in church. The church shouldn't be His tomb. It often looks like it is, though.

You would think some congregations were sitting around His coffin.

What people want from the pulpit is more than neat pulpit essays. We are not called to deliver sermons, but to deliver people. *People* are His concern. 'I have come to set the captive free.' He didn't come to renovate the prison cells or to make them more comfortable, with nice beds and colour televisions. He wants people out. The gospel is neither renovation, decoration nor reformation, but liberation.

Praise God, that is how it still works! Hundreds of millions all over the world are witnesses. They testify, 'The gospel has happened to me.' News!

How to have the original power

In earlier centuries in Europe, there was a most curious trade: the selling of relics. People hawked grisly skeletons and various other items which they claimed belonged to saints. Some of them were outrageous, such as one of Noah's teeth, or the iron filings from Peter's chains in prison. But behind it all was the pathetic longing to touch God's reality and power. They had no idea how to do so. They tried to do it second hand, through the bones and relics of apostles, martyrs and saints. They hoped these believers' blessings would brush off on them.

But why bother? The real thing is available first hand. If we do what the apostles did, we can receive what the apostles received. Peter himself said so (Acts 2:38–39). We all can know His power, and go forth garbed with Holy Ghost might. The original brand! For Paul it meant 'to make the Gentiles obedient, by word and deed, through mighty signs and wonders, by the power of the Spirit of God...I have fully preached the gospel of Christ' (Rom 15:18–19).

'They shall not teach every man his neighbour...saying, Know the Lord: for all shall know me, from the least to the greatest' (Heb 8:11). Pentecost is for repetition in each life. The apostles were not extraordinary people, but ordinary people with an extraordinary God.

How to plunder hell and populate heaven

For over six years, I ran a Bible correspondence school. That was in Lesotho, Africa, from 1968–1974. The purpose was, of course, to reach the lost people of the country for Christ. The enrollment grew to approximately 50,000 students.

To keep this project going put great demands on my faith. I was only a missionary. I needed an office, and the monthly rent was only $30. But one day I couldn't pay, and I prayed and groaned all day, 'Dear Lord, let me have $30 to pay the rent.' The hours passed, evening came, but I still had no money. Slowly, I walked down the road to the house where we stayed as a family.

Suddenly, in the middle of that road, the power of the Lord came upon me. I heard His voice clearly inside my heart, 'Do you want Me to give you one million dollars?' One million dollars! My heart raced the Formula One circuit. What I could do with that amount of money! Why, with one million I could bombard the whole world with the gospel, I thought.

But then, a different thought struck me. I am not at all a weepy person, but tears began running from my eyes, and I cried, 'No, Lord, don't give me one million dollars. I want more than that. Give me one million souls. One million souls less in hell and one million more in heaven— that shall be the purpose of my life.'

Then the Holy Spirit quietly whispered into my very spirit words I had never heard before—'You will plunder hell and populate heaven for Calvary's sake.' That day, a determination gripped me. I knew God had greater plans for my life, and I set out to fulfil them in progressive stages. God has granted me ever-increasing blessing and grace.

How often since then have I seen the devastating power of the gospel crash against the gates of hell, storming the dark domains of Satan. I often saw, within one week, 300,000 precious people respond to the call of salvation in our gospel crusades. I joked with my co-workers: 'If Jesus keeps on saving souls at this rate, one day the Devil is going to sit alone in hell.' I'm glad to make Satan sorry.

Knowing the power of the gospel, we don't need to be frantic. Jesus is equal to the need. The world is sick, and Jesus has the only remedy—the gospel. Our part is simply that we must carry this medicine to the patients. Jesus commanded it—'Go ye!' That is not a suggestion or a recommendation, but an order. We had better obey, or else miss the greatest joy known to man.

How to have an effective gospel

The message is Jesus. What He does shows who He is. The former is all-important. Jesus saves from sin. We are not moralising. We are not giving descriptions of sin. An American President went to church one day, and later his wife asked him what the preacher's sermon was about. 'It was about sin,' he replied. 'And what did he say about sin?' his wife enquired. 'Oh, he was against it,' the President told her.

People expect that. The question is: What can be done about it? People need victory over sin in their personal lives. They need to feel clean, forgiven. Many a man will tell you he knows he's not going to heaven, but he has no idea what to do.

We must major on how to get people out of the mire, how to get them cleansed by the precious blood of Jesus, how to receive assurance and the witness of the Holy Spirit. These are mighty themes.

I constantly stand before vast crowds. To say anything less than the gospel would be wicked. Thank God I have a gospel, a positive message of power and hope. Then I find the fountain of the love of God springing up. Healing waters flow in all directions. That love touches human hearts. Men and women open up to God. They often have little of this world's good things, but it matters less when they possess the riches of God: assurance, peace and joy which no factory makes, no shop sells, no affluence provides.

We are Christ's ambassadors. The gospel is a confrontation of God with sinners. Don't reduce it to a pleasant introduction. Our message carries the highest prestige. We have a word from the King. It has prior urgency. The gospel preacher is not an errand boy bringing a sealed letter, but one who has spoken to the King and understands the King's mind. It is not a message for anybody who happens to be within earshot. The gospel is not sent only to people who have had a previous religious interest. It is for all, high and low, without favour. God is saying, 'I speak,' and sinners should reply, 'I am listening.'

The gospel is not a proposition or suggestion. It is not thinking aloud, or an ongoing discussion. Preaching the gospel does not mean setting forth the orthodox faith in a nice address, like an actor's soliloquy to an empty stage. It is not an alternative, but an ultimatum from the King— from God. 'Believe or perish,' because 'God now commandeth all men everywhere to repent' (Acts 17:30). That is what Paul asserted. His hearers were the lofty and proud Athenian intellectuals. But Paul showed them that God the unknown was drawing near to them in love, stretching out His arms in welcome. The Holy Spirit takes the word and points it as a sword straight at every individual. Doctrinal study is not the same thing. The gospel is God's 'I', speaking to our 'I', as a personal communication. When the gospel is preached, it becomes a confrontation between the Lord and sinners, God stretching out His arms of love.

Next, we proclaim Jesus Christ the Healer. For us, our model is the Lord who proclaimed liberty and showed what that liberty was by healing the sick. The gospel is not a defence of God. God defends us, hapless victims of the Devil that we are without Him. Deliverance includes divine, miraculous healing. Some have thought healing was an incidental result, a mere attachment to the gospel.

Never! It is an ingredient of the message. We preach a whole gospel for the whole man. Physical health is part of the whole package. It is God's special offer.

The gospel is a miracle itself, and you cannot take the miraculous out of it. To preach a no-miracle gospel results in the creation of miracle-free zones, which, regretfully, some churches are.

It is not addressed to guilty spirits, but to guilty men and women, suffering in their bodies for their sins. Jesus forgives and heals as part of the process. This is how it is preached in 'the power and demonstration of the Spirit'. Otherwise, how can the gospel be a demonstration of power if it is all spiritual and not physical? Christ is the Healer, and His healing extends in every direction— towards soul, body, mind, circumstances.

Healing includes the authority to cast out demons. Demons may sometimes be directly behind sickness and depression. Not every sickness or weakness is demonic. Jesus made that distinction clear: 'Cast out devils, heal the sick….' The anointing of God rested upon Jesus to heal the sick, and the anointing of God rests upon His servants today for the same purpose, of course. It is wrong to underemphasise the healing of the sick, and it is wrong to overemphasise it. One can always fall from two sides of a horse. Some evangelists preach only healing. Certainly, wonderful things happen wherever there is faith, but people do not hear the message of salvation from sin. What use is it for people to be whole in body, only to be cast into hell? That is why, in our ministry, I am not speaking of 'healing crusades' but of gospel crusades. If we put all the weight on one side of the ship, it will keel over. To preach a non-healing Jesus is to present a non-biblical Jesus, just as much as if we did not preach a saving Jesus.

The third ingredient is Jesus, the Baptiser into the Spirit. Jesus the Baptist—but in fire, not in water. He is not just a tongues giver, or a spiritual gifts giver. He sends the Holy Spirit. In all our crusades, we pray for people to be baptised into the Spirit. I am not ashamed of this mighty blessing. I don't keep it dark 'until people understand'. It is part of the gospel, and I am not ashamed of the gospel of Christ. The apostle Peter preached the whole gospel in his first sermon, including the gift of the Spirit, and so do I. The Day of Pentecost was not just evangelical. It was charismatic as well! As long as the church emphasises the baptism in the Spirit, the Holy Spirit will stimulate evangelism and missions. As a flower carries in its blossom the seeds for new plants, so Holy Spirit evangelism carries in itself the seeds of its own perpetuity and increase.

The grand finale and the new beginning

The statesmen and world leaders do not know what to do, despite all the knowledge and wisdom of this latter day. Believers know. The full gospel sees Jesus today, striding the continents to conquer. He will ride on in majesty, the majesty with which He was crowned at Calvary, until He is King of kings and Lord of lords. He is now absent in body only. 'This same Jesus' that we must preach will return. All little kings, lords and rulers will be pushed aside, and the world itself will be lighted with His excellent glory.

When believers come together now, they enjoy His presence, but the world is insensitive and dead to it. Soon He will come, though, and all the world will know He is here again. He belongs here. He was born here, He lived here and He died here. He will come again to where He belongs, to His own. This time, they will receive Him.

This puts all His work together. We cannot leave it out of our message. For a warring, stricken, frightened world, this message is the only one to spell out hope. Jesus is the hope of the world. We challenge the world. 'Tell us,' we ask, 'how you think everything will be in peace. How do you think you will end up?' The world has no answer, no alternative. Let the world be ashamed, not us. Unbelievers have no hope. We have—Jesus. Preach Him. The world needs Him.

8

When the Miracle Stopped

Apostolic task

If Jesus were to walk the land today, and ask for volunteers to sign up as His apostles, there would be no shortage of applicants. Apostle is a noble title. But how many would want to be an apostle if they knew what they really had to do?

I do not think apostleship involved sitting at a managing director's desk. They didn't just sit. Apostle means 'sent one'. What were they sent to do? First, they were sent to be evangelists. Secondly, to suffer for it. Let me tell you—to witness and to evangelise is our privilege. We are doing what the apostles did.

The Lord appointed the twelve as His first witnesses. They were sent to introduce the gospel to the world, and our task is to follow on. Their distinction as apostles was to initiate all evangelism. Jesus gave them His teaching and they gave it to us. They were the foundation. We tread where they led.

'Apostle' was not a title of honour to make them famous. It described what they should *do* (ie, go)—and that they were also to be prime targets for persecution, not for prestige. We read 'God hath set forth us the apostles last, as it were appointed to death' (1 Cor 4:9).

They were not divinely-appointed church bosses. They left management to others. In Acts 15, the man who did that kind of thing, James, was not an apostle, because James the apostle had been martyred already in Acts 12. We read nothing about apostles giving out orders. Their special honour was that 'they were counted worthy to suffer shame for his name', and they rejoiced (Acts 5:41). Suffering as pioneers of Christ was the only high status they enjoyed.

In Mark's Gospel, the title of 'apostle' was used because they carried out a preaching and healing itinerary. Constantly, throughout the whole of the New Testament, apostleship meant one thing—preaching the gospel. Paul said, 'Christ...sent me to preach the gospel.' He began his great letter to the Romans with the clear statement of an apostle's work: 'Paul, a servant of Jesus Christ, called to be an apostle, separated unto the gospel of God' (1:1).

This was their area of authority. When Philip preached in Samaria and others evangelised in Antioch, the apostles felt they had to give it their approval, as custodians of the truth (Acts 8:14; 10:22). Jesus told them: 'I will give unto thee the keys of the kingdom of heaven: and whatsoever thou shalt bind on earth shall be bound in heaven: and whatsoever thou shalt loose on earth shall be loosed in heaven' (Mt 16:19).

Peter is not jingling his bunch of keys at the gate of heaven, as some kind of celestial receptionist or commissionaire. That is nonsense. The figure of speech Jesus used simply meant that Peter was to be the first to preach the gospel on the Day of Pentecost, thereby opening the kingdom to those who believe. Peter's keys were the gospel.

Indeed, the Lord made it quite clear that the keys were not exclusively in Peter's hands (Acts 1:8). The promise concerning binding and loosing was to all who believe and.

obey (Mt 18:18). The loosing power is by the proclamation of the word of God.

The apostles felt they were honoured to carry out the task of evangelism. It was a sacred trust. They were responsible for a royal treasure. Paul wrote of 'the glorious gospel of the blessed God, which was committed to my trust. And I thank Christ Jesus our Lord, who hath enabled me, for that he counted me faithful, putting me into the ministry' (1 Tim 1:11–12). He also declared that he was 'Paul...an apostle of Jesus...[who] hath in due times manifested his word through preaching, which is committed unto me according to the commandment of God our Saviour' (Tit 1:1–3).

So then, every apostle was an evangelist, first and foremost. But not every evangelist was an apostle. They are distinguished in Scripture each time the word 'evangelist' is mentioned (Acts 21:8; Eph 4:11; 2 Tim 4:5). But evangelists share the chief privilege of the apostle in preaching. They do the apostle's major task. Evangelists are an extension of the apostolic arm.

He made room for us

The apostles thought of their task as far more than just a particular job. It was the same work as the Lord Himself was doing. They were not only 'workers together' with one another, but 'workers together with Him' (2 Cor 5:20; 6:1). Partners with Jesus! Part of the heavenly crusade team of the Father, the Son and the Spirit. The work of God Himself is world redemption, and the apostles were called to participate. So are we. God made room for ordinary men.

On their first mission, they jealously stopped anyone else from doing anything, but Jesus reproved them (Lk 9:49–50). Even later, they thought they had an apostolic monopoly on evangelism. But they had to recognise the ministries of Stephen, Paul and the rest. These evangelists were in true apostolic succession. It is a strange apostleship which does not evangelise. It is a strange apostolic succession which does not carry out the specific apostolic task of preaching the gospel.

I would like to tell you how the Lord made room for me, also. I felt the Holy Spirit was urging me to visit a certain city. There were two churches there, so I wrote and asked for their co-operation. I received positive replies immediately. I did subsequently hear some negative rumours, but I left this with the Lord in prayer and remained confident that I should go. Nine months later, my wife and I arrived the day before the planned gospel crusade. We met the ministers to discuss arrangements with them.

I can think of some things which would have been more useful than this discussion. We went around in circles, no matter how I attempted to guide the conversation into more profitable directions.

Discouraged and sad, my wife and I eventually went back to our hotel and had a little rest. I must have fallen asleep as soon as my head touched the pillow, for immediately God gave me a vivid dream. It was a parable. I saw myself with the same two ministers in a sports field, of all places, and doing the last thing that would have entered into my head to do—the long jump. One of these ministers tried first, ran and jumped, but did not do too well. The other followed and did much better. It was then my turn. I began the run. As I ran, I felt something wonderful. An invisible hand went underneath me and lifted me. I sailed gracefully through the air. My limbs were moving as if they were running, but my feet did not touch the ground and my speed was terrific. Then I touched the jump line and ju-u-u-mped. There I was, landing at the very end of the sandpit. Marvellous! An Olympic record! When I looked back, the other two men were far behind. In my dream, I threw my arms high with great excitement, shouting, 'Oh, my God, you have made room for me!' I woke myself up shouting it.

This dream brought me great comfort by the Holy Spirit, and I have drawn encouragement from it ever since. God makes room for us. Bless His name! When He sends us on His service, He opens doors for us. We can go. We may have to take a daring leap, as in my dream, but we can take the long jump as the hand of God upholds us. We shall land where He wants us. We'll get there.

Filling all empty vessels

Now, I shall stress later that we must all work together within the church. Churches may not want to make room for evangelists sometimes. But I knew I must work with the churches. If I carried on independently, people might not see all that was involved. They possibly would think, 'This is easy for him. He's responsible to no one. He is not accountable to anybody who might approve or disapprove of what he does.' So I wanted to get the co-operation of the churches.

That is one thing. There is something else, too, which I will explain. Here is a key scripture. It is the familiar story of the never-failing cruze of oil (2 Kings 4:3–6). I would like to examine it. It will unlock some of the important principles of working with God:

> [Elisha] said, 'Go, borrow thee vessels abroad of all thy neighbours, even empty vessels; borrow not a few....' So she went from him, and shut the door upon her and upon her sons, who brought the vessels to her; and she poured out. And...when the vessels were full, that she said unto her son, 'Bring me yet a vessel.' And he said to her, 'There is not a vessel more.' And the oil stayed.

For many years my wife and I worked within the framework of a single denomination. God blessed us and used our evangelistic endeavours. Our gospel crusades began to grow. Then, through this key scripture, the Holy Spirit showed me what to do. I saw that the oil did not only fill the woman's own dishes, pans, jars and bottles, but the neighbours' vessels as well.

The Lord said, 'I do not have a burden for the empty vessels in your own house only (ie, my denomination), but also for the empty vessels in your neighbours' houses. Go and collect them and fill their vessels, too.'

'Oh,' I replied, 'my neighbours would never let me have their empty vessels. They would think that I wanted to steal them.' I knew pastors were nervous about other preachers drawing people after them; 'sheep stealing', as it were. The Lord answered, 'Build up an atmosphere of trust. Then they will lend you their vessels to fill.'

That early morning meeting with the Lord changed my whole perspective. In fact, it changed my direction. A burden rested upon me for churches outside the denomination to which I belonged.

But a man should never become a law unto himself, whatever his stature, place or work. 'The eye cannot say to the hand I have no need of you,' much less can a hand tell the whole body it can manage on its own. Even the apostles did not have that attitude.

Every worker needs the church like a fisherman needs the boat. The evangelist cannot sail away in waters of his own. God has set evangelists in the church. An evangelist may find himself blessed and financially independent, but that does not mean he should sing a solo without the back-up of the church. He should not impatiently shrug every hand from his shoulder, no matter how he burns to win the world for God.

Instructed by heaven to be instructed on earth

Take the case of that great servant Paul. As Saul, making his way to Damascus, from the very throne of God a voice spoke. He recognised that this was a divine visitation. With his deep religious interests as 'a Hebrew of the Hebrews' brought up at the feet of the great Rabbi Gamaliel, he must have wished a thousand times for such direct contact with heaven. In his enquiring mind so many questions simmered. And now the moment of truth had come, what would he learn? What revelations of the will and purpose of God were about to be his?

In fact he was told nothing. Nothing that is except, 'Arise, and go into the city, and it shall be told thee there what thou must do.' (v 6) In the city!

In the city were those he had come to haul off to prison for their 'heresy' of faith in Jesus as the Christ. Now he was sent to them because he needed them and was to become one of them. His first instruction would come from *them*, not by angels or voices from heaven. He learned his first Christian truth, that believers are not a sackful of random elements, but a living body, the church, and God did not allow him to by-pass it. 'Go into the city.' The Lord made sure of his earthly linkage.

Paul went, and submitted to the ministrations of others. We might learn from this man's wisdom and humility. A flash of light from heaven, an illumination of soul, a revelation of truth, and some men and women go off on an ego trip, independent of all counsel or oversight. They think they need not bother about those 'in the city'. But they should be wiser, for in the city 'there they will be told', and helped. Paul took the right direction from the beginning of his Christian life, and the church of his fellow-believers became strength and wisdom to him, as he to them. The result is history—glorious history.

In fact, we are all dependent upon one another, and if the evangelist needs the churches, the churches need the evangelist. The hand needs the body and the body needs the hand. We complement one another, as do husband and wife. If churches ignore the evangelist, they shackle him. If the evangelist ignores the church, he is throwing out a lifebelt with no lifeline attached.

This is what I learned that morning. So, knowing God's call, I consulted my denominational leaders, and shared God's vision with them. God gave me favour. They were in gracious harmony with me, and with their blessing I was released for evangelism beyond their borders and across all denominational frontiers. From that time onwards, I truly can testify that I have seen the oil of the Holy Spirit fill many vessels and very many churches, bringing multitudes of precious men and women to know Jesus. To God be the glory!

When the miracle stopped

The widow's oil miracle eventually stopped. Why? Did God say, 'That's enough for you today. I can't go on indefinitely'? He certainly did not. He was still pouring when they could find no more vessels. The widow said, 'Quick, bring me some more bowls or jars from anywhere. There seems to be no end to this,' but God outdid their capacity to receive. Then the miracle ended.

There will always be oil. Zechariah saw a golden lamp which never went out, because oil for it flowed through pipes coming directly from the olive tree (Zech 4). In the Holy Spirit, we have the source of all we need. As long as there are empty hearts, and as long as we go where God wishes and no one restricts our movements, the oil will keep on flowing, always and for ever.

Some people are baptised in the Holy Spirit and they worry that the experience will be temporary, the oil ceasing. The anointing abides for ever (1 Jn 2:27). But if we operate only with the vessels in our own little kitchen, the flow will cease. It is no use praying for an outpouring of the Spirit, week after week, just for our own small church, when the whole world lies outside, waiting to be filled. 'There is that scattereth, and yet increaseth,' proclaims Proverbs 11:24. Every church should see its walls to be as wide as the globe, and its roof covering all people on earth. Call the worldwide revival your revival! The scope of the local church can be universal, when the assembly works alongside men whom God has given to the universal church. Such a church will flow with Holy Spirit blessing.

If we shut ourselves in, and have nothing to do with

those God has set in the church, evangelists, we shall be
out of the swim, out of the river of God. An assembly
should not be a private club. Cologne Cathedral has a
notice for tourists which reads: 'This church is not a
museum.' What every church should be is a mission sta-
tion.

Teaspooners

In my imagination, I think of the sons of the woman in
Israel as they hurried down the streets asking everybody,
'Have you a jar, or a dish, or anything we can borrow to
put oil in, please?' Back and forth they went. Maybe some
carping soul complained, 'How many more things are you
borrowing? What are you and your mother up to?' I
wonder if anyone refused to lend them something to put
oil in? If they didn't lend anything, they helped to stop the
flow. Such selfishness stopped the miracle. We can help
the miracle of revival blessing, or we can limit it to our
little kitchen.

It is necessary for all of us to work with others. Some
may criticise, but we must not be put off nonetheless. The
widow's lads just smiled, knowing what their mother had
in mind, and continued borrowing bowls for the oil.

God means to anoint us, not with a smear of oil, but
with rivers of oil. When Jesus made wine at Cana, he
didn't fill a few glasses, but made about 1,200 pints—
enough to keep them in wine for weeks; enough to bathe in
wine if they wished; so much that the bridal couple didn't
know what to do with it all. Jesus fed the multitudes and
had twelve baskets full of leftovers.

If an over-cautious church won't assist because evangelists could run off with their vessels, there will be no
abundance for them. Ever since I have obeyed the voice of
the Spirit, we have seen abundance. I, 'being sent forth by
the Holy Spirit', began to work in harmony with the whole
body of Christ. It was like opening the sluice gates of a
dam, and we have all shared in the flowing and endless

waters of the river of God. Once we begin to calculate and
protect our own little patch, the river is diverted. Insular
people become isolated. Do we want floods of blessing?
Then let the river overflow.

The evangelist's initiative

Sometimes one has real enemies, raised up by Satan. It is
demonic opposition. Then the anointing of God 'breaks
the yoke' and that anointing is the protection of God's
servants. Often, carrying the battle right inside the gates
of the Enemy, I have realised that I am ringed about by
the Devil's forces, but those evil legions have also been
surrounded—by the angels of God. I know that if the
anointing were lifted, these forces would be upon me like a
pack of wolves, ready to devour me in minutes. Enemies,
critics, discouragers, they will come, but the anointed man
is undefeatable.

The Devil is as a roaring lion, we read, which reminds
me of the roaring lion that crouched to devour Samson.
Samson met this young predator on his way to Timnath
(Judg 14:5–6). The lion didn't know Samson, the
anointed judge of Israel. It had the surprise of its life—its
last surprise, as it happened. A lion's snarl usually terrifies
human beings, and they turn and run. Then they are
easily caught. But when Samson heard the snarls, something happened about which the lion knew nothing. 'The
spirit of the Lord came mightily upon him' (Judg 14:6).

When the Spirit of the Lord comes upon men, new
things begin to happen. People begin to resist the Devil,
and he flees from them. Are you timid? By the Spirit, you
shall be bold. We are like sheep among wolves, but the
sheep are on the attack. We have power to tread upon
scorpions, to walk the stormy waves. Experiencing the
Spirit makes us more than a match for doubt and intellect.
When we live in Him, we possess command, put demons
to flight and bring deliverance for body, soul and spirit.

So Samson, the lion's intended victim, did not flee.

Chasing fleeing victims gives lions an appetite for breakfast. But this man turned on the lion.

The ferocious beast found himself facing a ferocious man. Snarling over his shoulder, the lion tried to slink off, but it was too late. Mighty hands lifted him. Later, his carcass became a beehive. Samson, with his bare hands, 'rent him as he would have rent a kid'.

The church was never constructed for defensive purposes. The gates of hell should be invaded. Offence is the best defence. Instead of waiting to ward off the Devil's onslaught, turn the tide of battle and launch an invasion of the Devil's territory.

Jesus came into the world, not to defend heaven, but as a conquering man of war 'to destroy the works of the devil'. Christ took the battle into the Enemy's camp, invaded hell, relentlessly flushed out the foe, hunted him down, drove Satan into a corner, gave him neither quarter nor mercy, bruised that serpent's head and left him defeated and useless. Satan is not 'alive and well on planet earth'. Jesus has mortally wounded him.

That is what evangelism does, in the name of Jesus. Wherever the slimy trail of the serpent is, there the people of God should track the Devil down with swords whetted. Give him no rest, for we are 'more than conquerors through him that loveth us'. The best way to defend the truth is to declare it without compromise. We have not been called to apologise for what God has said, but to proclaim it. 'The sword of the Spirit is the word of God.' As David said of the sword with which he killed Goliath, 'There is none like that' (1 Sam 21:9). To defeat the Devil, preach the gospel. You'll never scare him off by shouting and noise. Use your sword.

Somebody once asked an evangelist, 'Why do you always preach on "Ye must be born again"?' He explained, 'Because ye must be born again.' No evangelist looks for a message to preach. 'Woe is me if I preach not the gospel.' He doesn't need to get together with other evangelists and say, 'Let's discuss what we should preach,' for all evangelists are totally without a doubt on that score. 'Repent and believe the gospel.' There is no point in reconsidering it, since there is no possibility of a better message. The evangelist is a man with a driving urgency, not a man with two minds. The gospel and nothing else on earth matters—neither fame, money, popularity nor life itself.

The evangelist's aim—I

The evangelist is a gift *to* the church (Eph 4:11) *for* the world (Lk 24:47). The true evangelist is not interested in building his own empire. His aim is two-fold. First and foremost, his work only makes sense in connection with the building of the local churches of Jesus Christ. Everything he does should have this as its goal: that people should be brought within the church, where the living word of God is preached. The greatest and even the most successful crusades almost become meaningless when they are not conducted within the context of the church and its growth. Crusades without local churches are only some kind of show, because the divine purpose is missing.

Jesus told us the story of the good Samaritan, a lesson for evangelists. A man fell among robbers while on his way from Jerusalem to Jericho. The Samaritan found him and cared for him. Other men, priests and religious folk, passed by. After attending to his wounds, with oil and wine, and lifting him on to his own transport, a donkey, the Samaritan took him to an inn. There, in the inn, he was nursed and strengthened (Lk 10:33–35).

After we have begun to lift fallen people who have been wounded in life, we need to get others to help. The Samaritan found such help at an inn, where the victim was strengthened and nursed back to health. The evangelist finds it in the church. There converts can be nurtured and built up in the faith. There they can become true disciples. Thank God for the inns along the road. Thank God for the evangelist who goes out to find the victims of the Devil. The church/inn caring for the convalescing new convert will have little business without the Samaritan/evangelist.

It is like fishing. During our gospel crusades, I always say that we, the evangelists, bring the nets and use the boats of the local churches. Together with them, we launch out and bring in a mighty draught of fish. Then we leave. We simply hand over the catch right there. We shake our nets out, repair and dry them, and go and lend a hand somewhere else. The evangelist gains nothing himself, except the joy and reward of seeing the kingdom of God built up all around.

The evangelist's aim — II

Secondly, the evangelist's aim is to proclaim. He proclaims the gospel, whether the people will or will not hear. 'And this gospel of the kingdom shall be preached in all the world for a witness unto all nations; and then shall the end come' (Mt 24:14). A local pastor cannot function in this way. God obviously depends on other servants. But everybody should be heart and soul with the man who has the vision and duty of proclamation.

Spiritual chemistry

To begin with, the gospel is only news if it is preached. It is only power if it is preached, also. Preaching the gospel is spiritual chemistry. Prayer brings power, but preaching releases it. Preaching the gospel is like plugging into a power socket. The gospel can't be used until it is spoken. Proclamation is absolutely part of the divine plan. People are saved no other way. This is the supernatural process. God instituted it for all mankind. 'It has pleased God by the foolishness of preaching to save.' It has pleased God that man should cast a net to draw fish from the sea, for fish normally won't jump ashore.

Jesus said, 'Bring of the fish which ye have now caught'

(Jn 21:10). First, catch them. Secondly, bring them. If churches never lift a finger except to let the evangelist preach, then do nothing to bring in what has been caught, the process the Lord intended has broken down and the circuit is cut.

However, as Christ indicated, in some villages the word will not be received, yet it still must be proclaimed. This Jesus illustrated with the parable of the sower. Not all sowings are equally successful, and some do not succeed at all. Why? There was nothing wrong with the seed (the word) nor with the sower (Christ Himself), but the trouble lay in where the seed happened to fall. In some places, it produced nothing because of the ground (Mt 10; 13:19–23). For the sower, the too-hard, infertile soil is frustrating. But don't be discouraged. Try somewhere else. Some preachers have no results because they preach discipleship to the lost, and the need to get saved to the already converted.

When a man works without results, he needs help, not criticism. Nothing succeeds like success in the worldly sense, and the successful in the church get the praise. But we have a calling to fulfil, and success is not always the test of whether such a calling is properly done. 'Preach the word; be instant in season, out of season; reprove, rebuke, exhort with all longsuffering and doctrine' (2 Tim 4:2).

Failure is not the rule, however. The Lord sent us to the harvest field so as not to waste our valuable labours on a concrete strip or on a desert. He means us to bring in the sheaves (Mt 10:14–15). Wait until the rains fall and the ground softens. Whatever comes, we must go into all the world and preach the gospel to every creature. Some will not hear, some will. When the gospel is preached in all the world for a witness, then Jesus will come, He said. The Lord of the harvest. So, to work. Let us hasten His coming.

PART THREE

Personal Drive

9

The Swimming Lesson

This chapter is being written just after we have returned from Yaoundé, a city of 435,000 and the capital of the Republic of Cameroon. There, a landslide for Jesus took place. A whole mountain came loose, in fact, with as many as 120,000 people in a single meeting.

This is all very exciting, of course, but how can we see the whole world effectively evangelised? The Lord must have visualised it as being possible, because He commanded us to 'teach all nations' (Mt 28:19). Nations! I am sure that God has big plans for reaching mankind. I go back again and again to the word, trying to understand this thought, and asking the Lord to open my eyes.

I once came to a familiar Scripture passage, much preached on, no doubt, but the Spirit of the Lord was upon me and the truth of this passage exploded in my soul. Do me the favour of reading Ezekiel 47:3−7 with me now.

And when the man that had the line in his hand went forth eastward, he measured a thousand cubits, and he brought me through the waters; the waters were to the ankles. Again he

measured a thousand, and brought me through the waters;
the waters were to the knees. Again he measured a thousand,
and brought me through; the waters were to the loins. Afterward he measured a thousand; and it was a river that I could
not pass over: for the waters were risen, waters to swim in, a
river that could not be passed over. And he said unto me, 'Son
of man, hast thou seen this?' Then he brought me, and caused
me to return to the brink of the river. Now when I had
returned, behold, at the bank of the river were very many
trees on the one side and on the other.

The first notable part of this passage took Ezekiel from
dry land into the waters of that glorious river, which,
many agree, is a picture of the life-giving flood of the Holy
Spirit. What an experience! From the dryness and dead-
ness of cold religion into the swirling reality of the Holy
Spirit. What an excitement to come to know this side of
salvation. This thrill is unique and inexplicable. No wonder the Charismatic/Pentecostal Movement is growing
stronger daily all over the world. In this remarkable
vision, the Lord has embedded lessons essential for us to
know if we do not wish to become spiritually stagnant.

God used an angel to lead the prophet Ezekiel. Four
times the angel carefully measured out 1,000 cubits, leading the man of God in stages. The first stage brought him
into the waters that were 'ankle deep'.

Ankle deep is God's minimum

Direct contact with the power of the Holy Spirit is absolutely wonderful, but do not forget that 'ankle deep' is
God's minimum! It is a tragedy that so many Christians
seem to park in this position. It is sound advice never to
follow a parked vehicle, because you will get nowhere.
Don't follow a parked pastor or a parked church member,
either. Don't settle down to God's minimum. No doubt
you can compare your experience with people who are not
even ankle deep, but compare your position not with what
is more shallow, but with the depth into which you can go.

Once I was invited to speak in a prayer meeting to people who did not believe in the baptism into the Holy Spirit. I did my best, but it was very difficult. The people just sat there, wordlessly looking at me with big eyes. A little prayer was said, and it was all over. When I left the gathering, I said to myself, 'It must be very difficult to swim in three inches of water.' This, unfortunately, is the condition of so many Christians. They paddle and work but make no progress, simply because they are grounded on the bottom. No wonder that things are so hard and wearing for them. Charles Haddon Spurgeon wrote that 'some Christians sail their boat in such low spiritual waters that the keel scrapes on the gravel all the way to heaven, instead of being carried on a floodtide'. What a nightmare.

There are many frustrated workers. They are devoted, almost working their fingers to the bone. Yet so little happens. Why? Because they are only rowing at the brink. They are 'do-it-yourself' people. They do the best they know how and then 'water it with prayer'.

That is not the way of Pentecost. Even Jesus said, 'The works I do, I do not of myself but the Father doeth them.' He insisted that we would do great works because He would send the Holy Spirit. He would do the work. The Lord does not hand us a toothpaste tube from which we might squeeze a little drop of power once or twice a day, just enough for our spiritual survival. The normal Christian life is this—'He shall be like a tree planted by the rivers of water' (Ps 1:3). Let me try to write a shout into this book: *the success of the Christian is in the fullness of the Holy Spirit.* By the grace of God, I have been shown the secret. Move into the deeper water of the Holy Spirit. Once in that floodstream, you will change immediately.

God's personal approach

There is something I must point out first. I asked the Lord to show me why the man with the measuring rod took

Ezekiel only 1,000 cubits at a time, in four stages. Why not take the plunge at 4,000 cubits all at once? The Holy Spirit showed me why. The Father is very understanding of each of His children. He doesn't 'throw us in at the deep end', all together and all at once. His work is lovingly individual. The angel was instructed to first 'measure' and then move. Our blessed Lord individually measures our capacity—and then leads. If Ezekiel had been led 4,000 cubits in one go, he would have drowned. But he made progress going into the deep in four stages. The Lord brings us along gently. He wants us to go, but not to rush in brashly. We should have neither cold feet nor hot heads.

Learning to swim

One day God said to me, 'Do you know what it means to swim?' Well, I'm a good swimmer, so I thought I knew. But did I? The Holy Spirit made me see something I didn't appreciate before. He said, 'When you are swimming you are in another element, and a new law operates. You have to let go and rest fully upon the waters of the river. Those waters carry you.'

I see that now. I am swimming in the Holy Ghost. His waters carry me. The Spirit lifts me. Swimming takes the weight off your feet. It gives your back a holiday and your joints go on vacation. He does the work. What, then, is the real handicap? The real handicap is to rely upon your own self. Depend on your own energy and ability, and you will be trudging along the river bank, right beside the very waters which could bear you in their bosom.

Many are working for God, when God wants to work for them. He doesn't want us to work so hard that we drop dead for Him. I saw a gravestone once with a man's name and epitaph. I read, 'His life only consisted of work,' and thought, that is an epitaph for a horse, not a human being. God didn't intend for us to be beasts of burden, or to labour like robots. He could create pack horses in abundance if that's what He wanted. But when the Lord thought of you and me, He had something in mind other than slaves. Our Father wanted sons and daughters with whom He could fellowship and feast at the table, sharing all He has with them. 'All that I have is thine' (Lk 15:31).

It is time to change the negative image of the Christian life. Do you feel that becoming a Christian has simply bowed you down? You never feel good enough. There's not enough prayer, or work, or love, or the Bible in your life, you feel. Duties throng you. But—you should be borne along by the Spirit in the glorious river of God. There are waters in which to swim. In Him, you are more than a conqueror.

We are like Joseph, who was taken out of a prison cell to rule. That is the principle of God's dealings all throughout Scripture. We are not to endure, but to enjoy our Christian life. I don't want to arrive in heaven to discover I had managed on 5% of what God wanted me to have. That's no virtue. I am interested in the other 95%. When it comes to the blessings of God, some people are as humble as peacocks with their false modesty. We need to understand the mind and the calling of God. As He led Ezekiel from minimum to maximum, so He will lead us if we allow Him to do so.

Life isn't a row of bean tins

Bible language has little of the sea in it. There is no nautical expression. Revelation 21:1 states, 'There was no more sea,' but Revelation 22:1 explains that 'he shewed me a pure river of water of life...proceeding out of the throne of God'. There lies the difference between a sea and a river. In Scripture, the sea stands for the masses of mankind and for the wicked, 'whose waters cast up mire and dirt' (Is 57:20). It is also the dumping-ground for all our sins. The same old water comes back day after day. The tide brings back the rubbish you thought had gone.

But the river is different. There's a constant freshness,

because it never has the same water. God has something new every morning. When the pop artist Andy Warhol painted a picture to represent the modern age, he mocked it with an exact representation of a row of identical canned beans. His work was biting satire. The world's diet is canned (or perhaps bottled) entertainment. There is not a single fresh item in the Devil's supermarket. And all the time God promises 'a land of rivers'. He puts us under His waterfall.

A river of power

Ezekiel swam and enjoyed it greatly. All who discover this secret will have their lives and ministries transformed. A few years ago, a completely frustrated minister of the gospel came to see me. He had just come from the psychiatrist and said that he no longer could carry the load of his church of fifty members. It was just too much. 'Are you baptised in the Holy Spirit?' I asked. 'No,' he replied, 'my denomination does not believe in it.'

I took time to explain to him this wonderful truth and prayed with him afterwards. In the evening he left, but he didn't really drive home, he *swam* home! God had done it. What can God's maximum actually be? I certainly don't claim to have arrived at God's maximum. But I am definitely in transition. I am going from 'faith to faith' and from 'glory to glory'. That is Holy Ghost progression.

The surprise that followed

After Ezekiel swam, he returned to the river bank. This is, in New Testament terms, no anti-climax, because once we have been in the river, the river is in us. 'From his innermost being shall flow rivers of living water' (Jn 7:38, NASB). This experience had transformed the prophet. But when he climbed the river bank, he looked and, wiping his eyes, cried out with astonishment: 'Behold, at the bank of the river were very many trees on the one side and on the other' (Ezek 47:7).

Why was that so special? Why did he wipe his eyes in wonder? He now saw something that wasn't there when he entered the river—trees! And this is the greatest truth of the chapter: while God changed Ezekiel in His river, the Lord changed the whole landscape around him at the same time. Conditions change with anointed people and an anointed church.

I suppose that Ezekiel had tried for many years to plant trees alongside the river and had failed dismally. He had even watered them with his own tears, yet the trees still perished. But now the Lord had done, within seconds, what Ezekiel hadn't been able to do in very many years. This is our faith for today! ' "Not by might, nor by power, but by my Spirit," saith the Lord of hosts.' People who flow in and with the Holy Spirit have reason to wipe their eyes every day, because the Lord is doing wonders. And, praise the Lord, nothing diminishes in God. Everything is getting more wonderful by the day.

Divine energy

Another notable detail is this: those very trees already bore ripe fruit. While Ezekiel had discovered the depth of the river of the Holy Spirit, God had planted and grown the trees in no time. He is the Creator of time and can shrink it whenever He wishes. 'And the fruit thereof shall be for meat' we read in verse 12. It was as if the fruit were beckoning him, calling, 'Ezekiel, come over here. No more cooking using your own recipe. God has spread the table for you. No more disasters in your kitchen. A balanced diet awaits you.'

How wonderful! All of a sudden, the man of God was, and is, in partnership with the Holy Spirit. No more scheming until we are steaming. No more groping in the dark. This is the wonder of a life and ministry in the Holy Spirit. This is how our world will be won for the Lord.

Holy Ghost evangelism will win our generation for God. It all begins when we are obedient to the promptings of the Holy Spirit and follow Him out into the depths, where there are waters in which to swim.

In our element

The Christian who is not in the river of the Holy Spirit is out of his element. We are not called to be desert dwellers, like the people of Israel were for forty years. The Lord had promised them a land of rivers. Christ has promised believers rivers, not as a rare exception, but as part of their natural environment. We are not to be bank sitters, admirers of the passing waters, but river men instead.

Many times people have told me that under their circumstances they could not live a victorious Christian life. One young man in Africa explained that his grandparents and his parents were all witchdoctors, and it was therefore impossible for him to live with Jesus in that place.

However, not one of us could be victorious anywhere in this sinful world, were it not for the Holy Spirit. Wherever we go, He is there. We move in Him and live in Him. He is our environment. We are baptised into Him. We are swimming in the river of God, not in a little pool He created for us that is one day likely to dry up.

To change the picture for a moment, we may just as well ask the question: 'Can a man live on the moon?' The answer is both 'No' and 'Yes'. He cannot live on the moon if he goes there as he is. But if he arrives on the moon with a proper space suit on, he can live there. The space suit contains the same air as that found on the earth. Wearing these space suits, the astronauts can walk, ride and jump upon the surface of the moon.

You cannot expect to live a successful Christian life if you are not in the Spirit, for that is how God arranged for you to live. Wherever we are, we can be in the Spirit, and that is the important fact. We can be on the moon physically, metamorphically speaking, but to sustain our life we breathe the air of heaven. Even in the worst places, foul with the breath of hell, we ourselves are enveloped in God. 'He that dwelleth in the secret place of the most high shall abide under the shadow of the Almighty' (Ps 91:1). He is our dwelling place, in every circumstance.

In our element of the Spirit we are unconquerable, invulnerable, going from victory to victory, our life hid with Christ in God. The man moving in the Spirit; the church moving in the Spirit; workers, evangelists, pastors and teachers moving in the Spirit—that is the only formula I know for success. In the Spirit of God, we can win the world for Jesus.

10

Passion Power

'The love of Christ constraineth me'

Love laws

On the lips of Jesus, the law becomes love. There are ten
commandments, but the first and the only commandment
for Him is, 'Thou shalt love the Lord thy God,' and 'the
second is like unto it'—'thy neighbour as thyself'. The
voice of Sinai yearns. Israel misunderstood God from the
start. Horeb thundered, but only with passion.

Love rights

Who really was this God, whose words burned themselves
into the very rocks? He identifies Himself, and establishes
His rights to give commandments. He has love rights. 'I
am the Lord thy God, which have brought thee out of the
land of Egypt, out of the house of bondage' (Exod 20:2).
That's who He is! His laws are love laws. The God who is a
'consuming fire' is one of compassion. He had come down

to deliver an ungrateful rabble of slaves from servitude.
He was set only on giving them nationhood and a new
country. Such a task would make great demands on His
inexhaustible patience.

The image of love

When God made man, I wonder if He might have shared
His eager thoughts with the angels? If He had, would
those spirits of wisdom have hesitated? 'Could Lucifer and
evil deceive them, and lead such frail creatures of flesh to
destroy one another?' the angels might have asked.

The God of all knowledge knew it would be. He knew
that the first man ever born would murder his brother.
But there was a master strategy. It would begin with Eve,
and continue with all women. Their very instinct would be
pre-programmed. Within their nature would be planted a
mother's heart; the purest form affection can take—an
affection which never seeks reward. It would filter through
to the family and set protective standards. Then the great
secret plan of God would slowly begin to develop and
work out, through all the ways and woes of Israel. At last
it would be unveiled, in the Son of His bosom. 'For God so
loved the world, that he gave his only begotten Son' (Jn
3:16).

His own image in man was the image of love, until the
storms of sin ruffled the waters and the reflection was
distorted. But God was not outwitted. He invested all He
had for everybody there was. The gospel blessed the ears
of men; the gospel was His heart, a revelation of troubled
anxiety for His creatures.

For us and to us

Evangelism is summed up in this—it is God loving us
through His gospel. Every message preached should be
winged with love. A man loving men by God's imparted
love. Impassioned men and women through the ages have

lived and died to preach Christ and His salvation to all tribes and nations. From the same divine force, the finest works of men have come: churches, charities, hospitals, orphanages, civilisation itself. The love of God in a man's soul is 100 times finer than every motive that has ever driven him.

When the presence of God had left Horeb, what was left? The first thing found is in Exodus 21:5–6: another love law. If a bond-servant married a wife, he could not legally take her away with him after he had served his contract with his master. He could keep his wife only if he stayed with his master in permanent servitude. Then his ear would be bored with a bradawl fastening him to the wood of the doorway. The scar would be there always, in the ear and in the door, and it would tell everybody, 'I love my wife and have given myself for her so I can give myself to her.'

Nothing other than love

That is the parable of the love affair of God with mankind. He gave Himself *for* us so that He could give Himself *to* us. God is love. That is what everything is about. That is why we were born; to love and be loved. To know the love of all loves is the secret of all secrets. Know that, and you possess the answer to the meaning of life. A loveless gospel is a contradiction—a sea without water, sun without light, honey without sweetness, bread without substance. The gospel is nothing other than love.

From Genesis to Revelation, the love epic moves from eternity to eternity. 'I have loved you with an everlasting love.' Hosea heard the cry of God. Israel was finally wandering into the darkness of their long historical night, and Hosea was permitted to catch the echo of the divine anguish. 'How shall I give thee up, Ephraim?...My repentings are kindled together' (Hos 11:8).

The only explanation given us when Jesus healed the sick, or did anything whatsoever, is always the same—He had compassion. Love is all there is to it. In fact, that is all there is to anything in God's universe.

Niagara of love

I don't suppose any angel ever asked the Lord why He proposed to make such creatures as we are, with our freedom to choose evil and the power to break His heart. The angels knew why. Whatever the pain, He had to pour Himself out in a Niagara of love. How better than upon those who could never deserve such a thing? What could better serve His purposes than enemies, the wicked, the oppressors and the oppressed seeking revenge? These are they who would be 'accepted in the Beloved'.

Hell is an awful and mysterious place. It is not a subject given us to enjoy. It is not for us to dangle men over the pit and see them squirm, simply because they are enemies of righteousness. We are told of this possible destiny of sinners in order to arouse our deepest pity and to drive us to care about and warn the heedless.

The love expression on His face

Jesus said more about hell than anybody, and, in fact, almost everything said about it in Scripture is something He said. One thing I would have wanted most powerfully is that I could have heard how He talked about hell. How did He say, 'Woe unto you...' even to the Pharisees? His accent, the look in His eyes, His gesture of agony for His creatures—no actor could imitate it, for it sprang from a divine heart too deep to fathom. Only His love shed in our hearts could possibly give our voices the pity of His warnings.

Love motive

If love was not the motive of the Son of God who came among us, what was? Look at these familiar words from

Scripture: 'Who for the joy that was set before him endured the cross, despising the shame' (Heb 12:2). Those who know best tell us that that word 'for' in 'for the joy', is a preposition better rendered 'instead of'. It does not mean 'to seek joy', but 'to sacrifice joy'. After the cross, He only regained what was His already. He, the thrice-blessed God, had exchanged His crown for a cross.

Again we read in John 13:1 that the time came for Jesus to 'depart out of this world'. But He didn't go. Instead, He took a towel and washed the feet of His disciples, and allowed Judas to go out and betray Him. He went all the way to Calvary, and became a ransom for all the Devil's captives. So John explained why: 'Having loved his own which were in the world, he loved them unto the end.' Jesus did not go back to the Father at the last minute.

Illustrating compassion

Let me tell you about that one word, 'compassion', in Scripture. It is the famous and unique word which is only used when God and Jesus are in mind. It means 'feelings toward the needy'. The following is one occasion when it is used.

There was a father who waited and waited, watching the road. One of his only two sons had gone, and had left his father and home to have a good time in a far country— silly fellow. That father was the Father. Day after day his eye had peered to the distant hill over which his boy might one day reappear. When that wonderful moment came, the father ran. *Ran!* I wonder if his running days had been over until that moment? But love drove the father to get to that boy before his son had a chance to change his mind and turn away from home. The father took ten steps for every one the son took.

What a story that is. The greatest ever told, except for the story of Jesus Himself. There is so much in it. For instance, that son had been working among pigs, and had returned home in the only clothes he had, the dirty rags that still carried the stench of the pigsty. But the father 'fell on his neck and kissed him'—embracing that smelly good-for-nothing. Affection overcame revulsion.

Love restores relationships

Is it so surprising that the elder of the two sons disowned this unwashed tramp? He said to the father with a sneer, 'This thy son....' The answer he got was, 'This thy brother....' Love restores all relationships. That's the gospel. The older brother accused the younger of wasting his money on prostitutes. This was his own supposition. It had not been mentioned before. But the father did not demand to know whether the allegation was true or false. He did not ask what his sins were. He only saw his son's plight. Here was a lost, dead man, now needing to be loved back into life. It would take time. He had come. That was all the prodigal could do, and now the father could forgive. This provided a chance for restoration. And there is the gospel, illustrating the word 'compassion'.

I understood this story better when I realised that the word 'compassion' implies a physical reaction. It has to do with the internal organs, when a feeling goes through our system and leaves us shocked inside. We say, 'My stomach turned over,' or, 'My heart stood still.' That is the word used to describe the feelings which disturbed Jesus when He gazed upon the people. He was moved with compassion. It was no mere condescending act of charity. It was the irresistible instinct in a mother or father to snatch a child back from danger. In a sense, He could not or would not help Himself. 'He saved others but Himself He cannot save.'

That and that alone accounts for the fact that He troubled Himself with universal sicknesses and the sea of human ills so long accepted as an unalterable fact of life. Ills seen sometimes even as the judgement of God. It is certainly true that many things resulted from His miraculous healings of the sick: the glory of God, the confirmation of His divine sonship, and so on. But that was not why He healed. His purpose in healing was to heal—simply that. I do not play the piano to prove that I have fingers, although that is also true, but because I love music. The purpose of music is music. The purpose of goodness is goodness. The consequences are mere side effects, quite incidental to His reason.

Jesus never exploited human suffering for His own glory. For that matter, what could He gain from His works of mercy? He did not need to come for his own profit. Why did He go to Bethesda, among that litter of humanity who were cast up like flotsam and jetsam on a forgotten shore? Why should He go to Nain to meet a dead man, or go anywhere, or come to earth at all, for that matter? There was no possible benefit or profit to Himself.

The truth is, He had a fatal attraction for the wretched. It led Him to a cruel death, but that was no consideration to Him. He would bring His healing touch to broken lives no matter what. We read that in the eyes of Jesus, the multitudes were as sheep without a shepherd and 'he had compassion on them and healed their sick'.

Then he called His disciples and sent them out to do a similar work. His work became their work—to show compassion. It was His compassion delivered by the disciples. But did they feel it? Do we? The disciples came back excited and thrilled because they discovered they had power, and that devils were subject to them. They did not mention those who had been delivered, and never referred to any satisfaction it gave them that precious men and women were now free.

If we are disappointed when the afflicted remain afflicted, so is Jesus. In fact, we would not feel like that at all if He did not Himself, for He made us that way. He heals to alleviate the consequences of sin, forgiving also the sin, for the same reason He saves. In no other way could He be satisfied. Deep satisfaction to the Lord is

loving, caring, saving, healing. He gets nothing else out of
it.

A furnace of love

God is a consuming fire. He is all love, a furnace burning
for His creatures. Whenever we carry the gospel, it must
be because we care. We are not to heal for the sake of
seeing a wonder. God is not in show business. He didn't
come to earth to make a name for Himself. If He did, His
audience only made a nail for Him.

He made trees, and men stripped them of their grace
and turned them into an ugly cross on which to exhibit
Him for their derision. He created man and thus Judas
Iscariot. The wood that bore Him, the iron that pierced
Him, the Judas that betrayed Him—He made them all
Himself in the beginning, knowing full well what their
uses would be. But He still made trees and He still made
iron for human benefit, whatever the eventual cost to
Himself.

Groundless love

Our own motives must be His. The love of God shed in
our hearts by the Holy Spirit makes it possible. He loves
us to love others. There may be imperfect motives behind
our ministry. In the end, our work will be tested as by fire,
and what was a performance for self will be hay, wood and
stubble, instead of the gold and silver jewellery of love.

Is there a hankering for miracle power, for display?
There is the occasional 'demon hunter' seeking exhibition
opportunities. Are there some who want to be known as
people of prayer, or as men of greath faith or spirituality?
Jesus said, 'They have their reward'—now, not in the
hereafter.

Love cannot have reasons. It is the ultimate. When
God spoke to Israel in Deuteronomy 7:7–8, He said He
had loved them for no reason. It was not because they

were a great nation, for they were smaller even than the peoples to be driven out of Canaan. The Lord told them He loved them because of His love for them—which is no reason at all. The reason for love is love, which is God Himself. Love is not God, but God is love.

Jesus amazes me. He healed the man at the pool of Bethesda and went away and never even said who He was. What advantage did that healing bring Him? No glory, no fame; in fact, it brought Him trouble and persecution (Jn 5). He took a deaf man, and led him by the hand outside the village so nobody would see, restoring his hearing. He did the same with a blind man. He restored others and told them not to say a word. There is only one explanation for His entire work, and that is that He loved people.

Profound compassion

To have His ministry is possible, but only to the degree of His compassion. A final consideration struck me. When Jesus stood at the tomb of Lazarus, why did He weep? I thought, 'But surely He knew there was going to be that greatest miracle, a rising from the dead? He ought to have had a radiant face.' But instead we read, 'He groaned in the spirit, and was troubled' (Jn 11:33). And in verse 33: 'Jesus wept.' Then said the Jews, 'Behold how he loved him!' (v 36). 'Jesus therefore again groaning in himself cometh to the grave' (v 38). Why?

The answer is that Jesus saw in this scene of sorrow the agony of all bereavements. Death did not merely affect His friend Lazarus. It was not for His own circumstances that He showed such deep feeling. 'He had no tears for his own griefs but sweat drops of blood for mine.' Jesus saw every funeral at that moment, and death, the king of terrors, haunting mankind. It was in that profound compassion that He went down into the caverns of death and conquered it.

That is the love, the gospel, and what, as the church, we are all about. This is the gospel the world awaits.

I I

The Anointed Unprofessional

There is a Bible episode that we hear over and over again as children. We hear it so many times we think that it is only 'kids' stuff', but it contains one of the most powerful words from God in all of Scripture. It is the story of the confrontation between David and the giant warrior, Goliath.

We must remember that we do not learn God's lessons with the head only. Our IQ has nothing to do with our spirituality. David had discovered truths as a mere lad. He was one of God's inspired spiritual geniuses.

There are general truths in this account of the amazing performance of David in the Valley of Elah. Here are key elements that are the very spears and swords of spiritual battle. We see that Christian work and warfare are illustrated in this famous episode. These are the truths by which victory is possible. They are not David's secrets, but the secrets of the Lord of Hosts.

I do not pretend that these points are hard to discern. However, merely to name the factors involved is not enough. I can do that right now. David's power lay in two equally important elements: faith and the anointing. But we cannot just leave it at that.

There are four kinds of people in this account, and I will make labels to identify them:

The anointed unprofessional—David
The unanointed professionals—Israel's worrying warriors
The ex-anointed professional—King Saul
The anti-anointed professionals—Goliath and the Philistines

The anointed unprofessional

David was not a professional warrior, but he was an anointed man. He didn't belong to the army of Israel. He didn't have anything to do with it at all. Scripture makes a point of telling us this. His job was back at home, minding sheep. He gate-crashed the whole army, an act of breathtaking audacity. But his anointing from God was his credential to do what he did. Actually, David originally only came to take a special treat from his dad and deliver a food hamper to his big brothers.

The anointed David, amazingly, was at this point an errand boy—an anointed errand boy. The Lord's anointed should be willing to be errand boys. If we are faithful in that which is least, the Lord will make us rulers over much. The anointing of God can rest on the humblest of workers.

David had never seen a battle, nor a battlefield, before he arrived in the Valley of Elah. He came with anointed vision and boundless faith in the Lord. Among the men of the army of Israel, however, he found only worrying warriors. Faith and victory were notably missing from the spirit of the army. He sensed grief and calamity.

The moment he opened his mouth to ask a question, he bumped into his eldest brother, Eliab. David was a seventeen-year-old youngster and Eliab was a professional, a captain in the army. Eliab was also the man Samuel had not anointed. He was an unanointed professional. He represented the whole army of unanointed professionals, and who knows how many today believe they are in God's army? Incidentally, Eliab had faith—of a kind—but we shall see that later.

There was bound to be friction between the anointed and the unanointed. David was like sandpaper to him— irritating. I want to point out some differences between these two classes, the Eliabs and the Davids.

Where the anointed and the unanointed differ

David saw Goliath and heard the blasphemies that came out of his mouth. Eliab listened with a sinking heart. Something different happened to David, though. The anointing of the Lord began to heat up within him. At the same moment, the hearts of Israel's unanointed professionals became ice-cold with fear. This has always been a notable distinction between the two, and it is still so today. Anointing gives great boldness, making people fearless. The anointing makes the difference between a correct, or academic, faith and a burning faith. Let me warn you, the one faith will always irritate the other. Don't be surprised. It's the old, old story.

Eliab undoubtedly had reason on his side. But it left him weighing up the balance of Israelite and Philistine forces. He saw no other resources. Eliab was able to make professional assessments of battle situations, and he saw that Israel had no chance of winning. David, in contrast, knew he had the God of Israel on his side, and felt holy stirrings and indignation within his soul. That was because of the anointing which gave him resources unknown to others. His inner eyes of faith were upon Jehovah. God's anointing upon him made him hungry for victory, excited by his eager anticipations. He did more than just hope and pray. That anointing was the 'earnest' of things to come.

Eliab was certainly a smart man. He had impressed even Samuel, the prophet. Samuel at first had thought that this man would make a fine king, but the Lord had said, 'Look not on his countenance or on the height of his stature: because I have refused him.' Why? We shall see.

In human eyes, David was not worth consideration—just the youngest, a bouncy teenager. He was like one of those that we would not choose even to give out the hymn books. But the Lord said, 'Arise, anoint him: for this is he!' A reddish-faced, unknown lad from the tribe of Judah. Being reddish suited the future king, as the jewel stone for Judah in the high priest's breastplate was red.

God's favour upon David had never given him favour with his seven unanointed brothers. Now, in the battle zone, Eliab spoke for all when he angrily asked David with whom he had left 'those few sheep in the wilderness'. David had not neglected his sheep. He had left them in the hands of a keeper. God's anointing does not allow anyone to neglect their proper duties. David was a man after God's own heart who did *all* God's will, even in the ordinary business of everyday duties. David, the anointed unprofessional, could not be bothered with Eliab's miserable quibbles—it was to him irrelevant nonsense.

The anointing of the Holy Spirit within him now reached boiling point. He ignored all mere protocol. If there was nobody to face Goliath, then he, a nobody, would face him. He would do it in the name of the Lord. The army considered David an outsider, but he was God's insider, nevertheless.

Face to face with the ex-anointed

Perhaps David opened his mouth too wide by questioning the army's policy. But the long and short of it was that he found himself in the tent of King Saul. Maybe it was a misunderstanding, but he said it was about time somebody faced the champion from Gath. The anointing, even more than David's faith, had made him speak out.

David recognised Goliath as his own enemy, not just as the army's target for the day. Here was the deadly foe of every man, woman and child in the land. Getting rid of him was everybody's business—army or no army.

That is true of the Devil today. The kingdom of God can't be run only by professionals paid out of church funds. Anointed unprofessionals are needed. The Devil is a menace to everyone.

A battle needs supplies and money, some of which David had come to bring, although money is no substitute for dedication. But David could not stand around any longer. For what was he anointed? Everyone knew something should be done, but who would do it? Eager hands pushed David forward. No doubt Goliath would make mincemeat of him, but it would break the deadlock. A nobody like David didn't matter. He could be offered as the sacrificial lamb. Then Israel could get on with the main battle. Let us now enter the tent of King Saul and see what happened.

It was obviously a joke to Saul and to his generals when a raw lad from the country came in and proposed to be the defender of Israel. But the fact is, when Samuel the prophet had anointed the shepherd boy David, King Saul had become the ex-anointed of the Lord. Now the anointed and the ex-anointed stood face to face. Saul looked at David with amusement. But David was quivering under a powerful Holy Spirit anointing. The ex-anointed had become the opinion leader of the unanointed—and nothing is more fatal than such a combination. Saul said, 'You can't fight Goliath! Do you know what you are up against? Have you seen how big he is? You don't know the first thing about combat. He has been a warrior all his life.'

There are always those who try to push others out, and always those who push others in to do what they don't fancy doing themselves. Eliab wanted to freeze David out, but you can't freeze fire. Saul wanted David to go in and fight instead of himself. If the army had voted, they would have been 99.9% against David, but David wasn't waiting to be democratically elected, nor was he thinking about popularity. Jesus said, 'How can ye believe, which receive honour one of another...?' (Jn 5:44).

The ex-anointed

Now, the captain of all the ex-anointed is the ex-anointed Satan, who was 'the anointed cherub that covereth'. This is quite an awesome fact, as we read in Ezekiel 28:14–15, 17:

> Thou art the anointed cherub that covereth; and I have set thee so: thou wast upon the holy mountain of God; thou hast walked up and down in the midst of the stones of fire. Thou wast perfect in thy ways from the day that thou wast created, till iniquity was found in thee...Thine heart was lifted up because of thy beauty, thou hast corrupted thy wisdom by reason of thy brightness: I will cast thee to the ground.

And Isaiah 14:12–14 adds:

> How art thou fallen from heaven, O Lucifer, son of the morning...For thou hast said in thine heart, I will ascend into heaven, I will exalt my throne above the stars of God...I will be like the most High.

Really, in a sense, the Devil had faith. According to James, 'The devils also believe, and tremble' (Jas 2:19). But the anointing had departed from Satan and left the evil husk of a once-illustrious being.

Now King Saul was a pathetic reflection of the same condition. Just as Satan pursued Jesus to kill him, Saul soon would be acting similarly, pursuing the anointed David. In both cases, a kingdom was at stake. The ex-anointed always will persecute the anointed of the Lord. Satan, not Jesus, 'thought it robbery to be equal with God' (compare Phil 2:6). But Jesus 'was obedient...even unto the death of the cross...therefore has God highly exalted him and given him a name that is above every name...'. Praise be to God for Jesus.

When David met Saul, he was undaunted. He had certainly never fought a professional soldier, but he had fought wild beasts. Predators were always after his flock. A bear and a lion had come and wished they hadn't when they met David. Goliath was a one-man war machine, a human tank, but in David's view he was too big a target to miss, and with God, David felt like a whole armoured division. 'For by thee I have run through a troop; and by my God have I leaped over a wall' (Ps 18:29).

With David it was all God—God or nothing. And it was God's honour Goliath challenged. Goliath had thrown down the gauntlet, not merely to men, or to the Israeli army. He 'had defied the armies of the living God'. That was Goliath's mistake, one, as it turned out for him, slightly more unhealthy than a headache. All David had to do was simply whatever had to be done. God would help David to succeed. Faith told him he could, and the anointing super-charged his eagerness to do so.

Saul's armour

Now Saul should have fought Goliath. He was head and shoulders above the biggest men in Israel, we are told. Furthermore, he was the king, the one who had known the Lord's anointing. And there was also mighty Abner. Instead, the two of them let David do it. In fact, the first thing Saul did, like unanointed professionals often do, was to make sly fun of this peasant lad who believed God could give him victory over the greatest warrior in the Philistine forces. In Saul's mind, David was naive. David, a deliverer? That was just absurd.

So King Saul smiled, winked at his brave general staff, and offered David the use of his own royal armour. That would be comical. What a figure David would cut; half Saul's size, parading in front of two armies in that over-sized equipment!

First, the leather coat. The shoulders, with layers of leather and bronze, stood out six inches from David's

body, burying him. The chain mail weighed him down.
The brass helmet...David turned his head sideways and
the helmet stayed forwards. The belt was a size 44, while
David's waist was only 29 inches. Saul's sword was so long
that it trailed on the ground and threatened to trip little
David. Goliath would die all right—of laughter!

When the anointing boils

What must Goliath's reaction have been? 'Give me a
man,' he had roared (1 Sam 17:10). He had waited for
Israel's answer. It would have to be their greatest man of
war, he surmised. Then, the hero finally came, emerging
from the ranks of Israel's mighty warriors. Goliath could
hardly believe his eyes when, with an uproar on both
sides, a stripling in sandals and a farmer's smock ran
across the field. His weapons were a couple of staves and a
little sling. Goliath felt it was a studied insult—did Israel
think they were only chasing off a dog, sending a lad with
sticks and à sling?

David's faith might have been evident in his being there
at all. But Goliath was also up against the very Spirit of
God. Invisible within the shepherd lad's heart, the anointing began to boil. There was no holding back any longer.
Note that 1 Samuel 17:48 says that David 'ran' towards the
Philistine champion, like an arrow released from the bow
of the Almighty God. The unanointed professionals
watched from a safe vantage point.

Goliath bellowed a hoarse warning at David. In contrast, came the voice of the sweet singer of Israel, the
musical tenor which later charmed Saul in his mad fits.
Maybe Eliab or some other scornful men shouted, 'Sing to
him, David—he might cry and go home.' The words
didn't charm Goliath.

Anyway, Israel's thousands were on their feet, watching and shouting. The soldiers had done a lot of shouting.
They were good at it. Rattling their spears on their
shields, hundreds of them made a frightening racket all

together. But Goliath was one of those stubborn facts that would not go away.

Mind you, if it was a matter of faith, they all had faith. David believed nothing more than they did. They had the Ark of the Covenant. Not only that, but the Israelites were God's chosen people. They sang about it. Chanted a Psalm, even— 'The Lord mighty in battle.' They stamped it out in rhythm until the ground shook. All that, but still nobody did any fighting. They had faith, but they did not act on it. The anointed David, however, felt the Spirit shaking him.

The army of the Lord—is it like that today? Does His army do everything except fight? Everything except evangelise? Israel spent time organising themselves, and that's all. They polished their weapons, argued about who should be the leaders, no doubt discussed the army's structure, policy and methods. The army of the Lord can be like that, chiefly concerned with polishing up the wherefores and therefores of their constitution, discussing church order, claiming to be 'a people of power', like Israel facing Goliath. But they do nothing actually aggressive for God, no real evangelism.

God's bullet

David did what any of those men should have, and certainly could have, done. He fought. Just that. But note: he turned his passive beliefs into active faith. Because he believed, he tackled the giant. He did not use professional weapons, but only what he was accustomed to: a sling and a stone. He could hit a hair at fifty paces, but facing a giant was another situation.

Now here is the crux of the matter. Don't mistake presumption for faith, and remember, to do God's work, you must have God's anointing. It is no coincidence that the only believer in the army to tackle the enemy was the one who carried the anointing of God.

That is what God wants—men of faith and anointing.

The anointed man will match his action to what he believes. That is the man whose faith will make him attempt the impossible, doing what he would never do unless he believed God. We can all do the ordinary things and trust God. David did the extraordinary thing and trusted God. That is what faith can be like when it comes with the anointing of the Spirit. We believe for the impossible, and do it.

I have no idea how hard a stone from a sling can hit. But I do know that when it is slung by an anointed slinger, it can travel like a bullet. That stone sank into Goliath's forehead, prostrating him, and the youthful victor administered the 'coup de grace' with Goliath's own sword.

Know this—your word, if it is His word, carries far more weight than all argument. It catches people where they are not protected. I rely upon it when preaching to thousands of people, all of whom are different. God knows best what word will reach them. The professional enemy had prepared for every danger, but not for a stone from a sling. God has many a surprise to spring on the Devil. He does not understand who, or what means, God is likely to choose. When we move in the Holy Spirit, we always find the Achilles' heel of the Devil and thus defeat him.

David, the anointed unprofessional, stuck to his brand of active faith and gloriously succeeded. Then all the brave, unanointed professionals of Israel took heart. They chased the Philistines, who were fleeing already. That must be some other kind of faith!

Finally: the anointed professional

It would be unfair not to mention the following. David soon became a 'professional' as well—an anointed professional. Anyone who does something long enough will qualify at some time. But, in spite of relying upon higher learning, old routines and rites, he kept a spiritual freshness through the Holy Spirit, as God said in Psalm 132:17–18: 'There will I make the horn of David to bud: I have ordained a lamp for mine anointed. His enemies will I clothe with shame: but upon himself shall his crown flourish.'

The 'lamp' was the Spirit of revelation, the Holy Spirit. David received new spiritual insight all the time. He relied upon the anointing of the Holy Spirit, and thus upon his Lord and God. God does not work miracles in order to save us trouble, but to glorify His name.

Believe. Act. Make sure of your anointing and say to the Lord, 'Now bid me run, and I will strive with things impossible.' God moves with the men who move.

12

The Pathetic King

Today, nations are being shaken by the power of God. This is not man's doing, but the work of God. However, people do ask, 'What is the secret of your success?' That, at least, is how they put it. The fact is that nothing can measure up to the effects of the gospel.

Entertainment, politics and other attractions may draw crowds, but nothing is like the gospel. It offers no cheap popularity, yet its wonderful power is bringing millions together in marvellous fellowship around the globe.

But how does it happen? The answer is: the kind of evangelism that wins the world is Holy Ghost evangelism, which makes use of the weapons God has given for this task, namely the gifts of the Spirit.

Anointed preaching, along with anointed music and singing, are not the only explanations for our success, I am sure. We must have those means, but the first disciples had even more. The New Testament talks about 'manifestations', which were things to see. They are truths made visible.

What are the works of God? They are not only conversions, or even healings. They include revelation, prophecy, supernatural knowledge, wisdom, discernment, dreams, visions and authority over the powers of Satan. Such are aspects of our crusades and meetings which I feel have helped to attract the hundreds of thousands. People wake up to the reality of spiritual things when they see something that is beyond mere words. The gifts of the Spirit supply this slice of experience.

In this chapter I want to stress the glorious possibilities of these weapons, the gifts. By these God-given means, the timid soul can become bold, and the defensive person can become aggressive. The Lord intends us to carry the credentials of an ambassador. To those whom He sends, He also gives this startling power and authority.

Let me take time to go into this subject. Many long for these spiritual gifts, but are perhaps nervous about using them. 'Suppose I am wrong?' they think. But the worst mistake is not to employ the weapons of the Lord. Remember some key scriptures. 'Be thou strong and very courageous' (Josh 1:7), the word states. 'In the fear of the Lord is strong confidence' (Prov 14:26). We can 'be strong in the grace that is in Christ Jesus' (2 Tim 2:1).

There is one Old Testament scripture that has fascinated me for a long time. Put alongside the New Testament truth, it gives a clear picture of how God does turn the tides and the tables on His enemies. Here is the passage:

And Joash the king of Israel came down unto him [Elisha], and wept over his face, and said, 'O my father, my father, the chariot of Israel, and the horsemen thereof.' And Elisha said unto him, 'Take bow and arrows.' And he took unto him bow and arrows. And he said to the king of Israel, 'Put thine hand upon the bow.' And he put his hand upon it: and Elisha put his hands upon the king's hands. And he said: 'Open the window eastward.' And he opened it. Then Elisha said, 'Shoot.' And he shot. And he said, 'The arrow of the Lord's deliverance, and the arrow of deliverance from Syria: for thou shalt smite the Syrians in Aphek, till thou hast consumed them' (2 Kings 13:14–17).

Cotton-wool comfort

Joash, the King of Israel, was young and inexperienced
when disaster threatened his kingdom. The Syrian army
had mobilised against him, and he knew he had nothing to
match it. He had visions of defeat and his own imprison-
ment. Even the possibility of death haunted him. He felt
sick with worry.

Joash was one of Israel's bad kings, but in his extremity
he remembered the Lord's prophet, Elisha, who was then
about eighty and likely to die soon. The King visited
Elisha. He approached him with flatteries. He described
Elisha's usefulness to Israel as like 'the chariot of Israel
and the horsemen thereof'. Then he 'wept over his face',
letting the old prophet see his tears, crying, 'O my father,
my father....' It was quite a show. The fact was, however,
that Joash wasn't weeping because Elisha was dying, but
because he might die himself.

Elisha simply told the king to take his bow and arrows.
I think that he could just as well have said, 'Take your
handkerchief.' Elisha had seen too much of Joash's ways
to be moved by his sob story.

Let me tell you—God was not impressed, either. It is
high time for somebody to say that God knows when people
are weeping only because they feel sorry for themselves.

There are a few who seem to need much more of other
people's time. In fact, this is sometimes because it is so
difficult to know what their trouble is, if indeed they know
it themselves. They may occasionally be victims of mental
bruising earlier in life.

Leaders who specialise in counselling may find such
patients give them plenty of practice. There is the danger
that the hours devoted to them could drive the trouble
deeper into their consciousness, even making such folk feel
they are very special sufferers, beyond the normal ability
of the Lord to help them. But nothing is too hard for God.

In a general way, the job we have is not to cotton-wool
people who may already feel too sorry for themselves. Our
aim is to wake them up, not lull them and give them

soothing pills. There is a moment for people to come out of themselves, and to see again the needs of a dying world. It would be sad if the valuable time which is given someone, without ever resolving their personality problems, took away from time which should be given to winning the lost.

Elisha would have none of it. He had no time to hunt for tissues for the King's eyes when national calamity loomed. He resorted to no probing enquiries. The need was plain. He saw the King's tears were not for a dying prophet, nor even for the nation, but for his own future. By the word of the Lord, therefore, without formalities for the royal presence, Elisha came straight to the point.

He said, 'Take bow and arrows.' He was brusque, perhaps, but when enemies are invading, the answer has to be just that—bow and arrows. A military attitude was needed. Joash must forget himself and be a real king to his people.

Trembling or triumphant saint?

Where are our weapons? Paul wrote, 'Stir up the gift of God which is in thee' (2 Tim 1:6). He instructed, 'Stir up.' The word Paul used has to do with fire, and it means 'to bring up to full flame'. Don't cool off. Use the fan on the dying embers.

Joash was a feeble king, as we shall see, with little fire in his bones. He went crying to Elisha, 'My father, my father,' when he was scared, instead of mustering his army and bringing weapons out of the armoury. Elisha would have appreciated action a lot more.

We have our weapons, and the Devil has done his best to stop believers from using them. When God opened His armoury and displayed the gifts of the Spirit at the beginning of the twentieth century, alarm bells rang in the church. The gifts described in 1 Corinthians 12–14 had been commonly interpreted as natural, not supernatural. There had to be a revision of biblical exposition. The church had long given pre-eminence to natural gifts and abilities. Valuable though they are, they can never take the place of the true miracle endowments of the Holy Spirit, and must not be confused with them.

Many churchmen and medical doctors have opposed divine healing. They have made much of those who are 'disappointed' and who are not healed immediately. They forget that doctors 'disappoint' millions. Nearly everyone in the graveyard has been to a doctor first. Some church folk who object to divine healing simply because some are not healed, themselves do not minister to the sick at all. This leaves everybody unhealed. Where is compassion, or obedience to the Scriptures?

Other gifts have also come under attack. When the word of knowledge was first being manifested by Pentecostal and charismatic evangelists, many declared it to be 'like spiritualism'. Why shouldn't God do such mighty things? In fact, spiritualism and clairvoyance are the horrible counterfeit of what God means to do. The gifts of the Holy Spirit are far greater than anything the occult can produce. There must be the real wherever there is the false.

Some Christians have let their bow and arrows gather dust in a corner because of such critics. Others have been hurt, perhaps by remarks from a fellow believer, and thus have dropped their gifts of prophecy, or of tongues and interpretation. They have 'lost' them, though God never takes them back, for 'the gifts and calling of God are without repentance' (Rom 11:29). These gifts *must* be recovered. This is the word of the Lord to such people. Go back to the day and to the place where you left those spiritual gifts, and ask the Lord to forgive you. Dry your tears of despair and 'take bow and arrows' again.

Waiting for God's moment

When I enter a meeting, I have my bow and arrows with me. The bow is already under tension, for I am praying in my heart, 'Lord, which is your appointed target? Where is the word of knowledge? In which direction is the anointing of the Holy Spirit flowing? Where is the key miracle for today?' That is what I mean—my bow is under tension, at the ready.

King Joash was a pathetic character, but he did take up his bow and arrows. He couldn't see properly, for his unmanly weeping. He was so scared by the enemy threat that his hands shook. But then, something happened that changed everything. 'And Elisha put his hands upon the king's hands.' Don't worry, God will do that for you as well. Like Ezra kept repeating, 'I was strengthened as the hand of the Lord my God was upon me' (Ezra 7:6, 9, 28, 8:18). Ezra wasn't the only one strengthened. The Bible is full of testimony of those 'strong in the Lord and the power of his might'. Glory to God. It is exciting.

Having the gifts, God's bow and arrows, is one thing. Using them is another. 'Prophets' should not just open their mouths because they are prophets. There is God's moment of command, that touch of God upon the hand. Have you heard the story of the elephant who found the nest of an ostrich? The mother ostrich had gone off to a river somewhere to drink. The elephant saw her eggs uncovered, and big elephant tears rolled down his trunk. 'How can a mother be so irresponsible and leave her eggs unprotected? Well, until she returns, I will help out.' So the elephant, with maternal concern, sat on the nest. The devastating result was scrambled eggs. He had a heart of compassion, but not a drop of wisdom in his elephant-sized brain. Are some Christians like him?

Joash had his weapons, and Elisha's touch imparted strength. The King dried his eyes, and fear left him. Divine confidence came. That same experience can be ours. It has been mine very many times. Suddenly, I will know that the Enemy will be beaten and his works destroyed. I am sure miraculous things will take place. The anointing is there, breaking the yoke. We can be 'strong in strength which God supplies through His eternal Son'.

'Open the window'

Elisha next told Joash, 'Open the window eastward.' So, you have the weapon gifts, you have the anointing. Now what? You can't shoot arrows through a closed window, so open it, begin to prepare and make opportunity. Set things up. Clear the decks for action. What I mean is, listen to the Holy Spirit in this matter, as Joash listened to Elisha. It may mean pushing aside normal arrangements, 'official channels' and even courtesies perhaps, but if God says it, do it—always remembering the elephant and the ostrich. When Jesus chooses, don't let anyone stop you (Jn 15:16).

I was about fifteen years of age when God first put His hands on mine and used me in a special way. I was in my pastor father's church prayer meeting in northern Germany. We were all kneeling when the power of God came over me and I felt as if my hands were filled with electricity. I clearly heard the Lord tell me, in my heart, 'Arise and lay your hands upon Sister C.' I nearly fainted thinking of the consequences, for my father was a very strict man. How could I just get up and put my hands on that lady? But when I hesitated, the Lord seemed to turn up the voltage, and I felt as if I were dying. Slowly, I lifted my head and peered around for Sister C. I kept down and crept to her so I would not be detected. Then I put my hands on her head. At that moment I felt the power of God go through my hands into her.

Father had seen me, however, and his face showed he was not pleased. He went straight to her and said, 'What did Reinhard do to you?' She replied, 'Oh! When Reinhard laid his hands on me, it was as if electricity flowed through my body—and I am healed!' By going to her as God commanded, I learned this lesson: 'Open the window....' When Joash had done that, the next command could be given.

Shoot!

One expected command was not given. Elisha did not say, 'Take aim.' There was nothing for which to aim. God wanted him to shoot, just shoot. The arrows of God are self-targeting, and they will never miss. They are like pre-programmed cruise missiles. They will strike, and no heart can avoid them.

When God gives a word of knowledge, I need not figure out whether it fits, or whether it is likely to be correct. God knows better than I know. My duty is to release the arrow from the bow, and it will become an 'arrow of deliverance'. The Spirit of God alone can plumb the depths of a man's own spirit. He will not slip up. The Spirit is familiar with everybody's history and with their most secret thoughts. For our rational minds, it is not always easy just to shoot through an open window of opportunity without seeing the actual target. When we do, though, the results are amazing.

One of the overwhelming experiences I had of this kind involved my brother Jürgen. We had grown up together as sons of godly parents, but he didn't want to follow Jesus. When we became adults, he had his career and life mapped out.

Time passed, and I did not know that his wife had left him and that his closest friend had died of cancer. His life became meaningless to him. Then one night he dreamed. He seemed to be walking on a high bridge when he slipped and felt himself falling, crying out. Then he awoke, drenched in perspiration.

Later he said, 'For the first time in my life, I had a burning desire to pray to God, remembering the scripture I had learned as a child, "Call upon me in the day of trouble: I will deliver thee" [Ps 50:15]. I went down on my knees and said, "Lord, You know that I do not even know that You exist, but my brother Reinhard is Your servant. Give me a sign through him that You are alive." ' That night, I was 10,000 kilometres away in Africa. I didn't know about his troubles, nor that he was considering ending his own life, for there was very little communication between us.

However, in the small hours of the morning, I had a terrible dream myself. I also saw a high bridge and my brother Jürgen walking on it in some kind of fog. The bridge had no guard rails, and I feared that Jürgen might lose his orientation and fall off. He walked on into that fog. I dreamed that I called out in desperation, '*Jürgen!*' The next sound I heard was that of a voice crying out from the bottomless depths. It was my brother's voice.

I then woke up, wet with perspiration, and asked, 'Lord, what is this?' He answered me. 'Jürgen is on the bridge to eternity. If you do not warn the godless, I will require his blood from your hands....' The fear of God came upon me. In brief, I wrote a letter to him. True, I had fierce battles in my own heart before doing so, but I told him of my dream. Also, I pleaded with him to receive Jesus Christ as his personal Saviour.

One day before Christmas in 1987, I received his reply. Jesus had wonderfully saved his soul. Hallelujah! He knew his sins were forgiven. He wrote, 'I am walking with the Lord every day. He has solved all my problems.' When I got that letter, I could not control my emotions, and I just wept for gladness.

How wonderful the Holy Spirit is! How effective are His gifts! They are God's powerful weapons. We play into the Devil's hands when we are shy about them or apologetic about their use. What if I had not written that letter? What if I never had opened the window eastward, shooting the arrow into the dark? I did not do it led by my rational decision, but the arrow nonetheless found its mark. In the name of Jesus, I say to you, 'Open your window. Push aside your fears. Let your obedience in faith overrule all your nervousness. Let go and let God have His wonderful way through you. And let your wisdom be not sensual but wisdom from heaven' (see James 4:15).

Joy

When Joash shot that arrow through the casement, something happened to Elisha. He shouted, 'The arrow of the Lord's deliverance from Syria: for thou shalt smite the Syrians in Aphek till thou hast consumed them' (v 17). Joash believed it, and went forth in the strength of that confidence. Three times he overcame the Syrians, recovering his lost cities of Israel (v 25).

One mighty meeting with God changed the course of that King. That is all it takes—one meeting with God. The men and women whom God uses have had such a meeting with Him. They have moved out of religious routine into the winds of the Holy Spirit. You can have that meeting, but you have to be desperate enough to break through. The essential thing is the anointing of God. Until you do, it is presumption. When you have His orders, it is presumption not to obey.

Boiling point

The story of Joash and Elisha is remarkable. What happened, as I have described here, gives us these great truths. But the fact is, there is still another facet to it. Joash could have done even better. We go on to read that the prophet Elisha told him to take his arrows now and 'smite upon the ground'. He did, three times, only half-heartedly. 'The man of God,' we read, 'was wroth with him, and said, Thou shouldest have smitten five or six times; then hadst thou smitten Syria till thou hadst consumed it: whereas now thou shalt smite Syria but thrice' (2 Kings 13:19).

Despite the prophet's hand on his, the King's weak-willed character showed through. Joash was not bold. Just three knocks on the ground was typical of a hazy temperament. A man of powerful personality would have done even that small job well, and would have smitten the ground thoroughly time after time, giving it a good hammering.

God loves vigorous souls who put everything they have into what they do, however small the command. No command of God is a matter of unimportance. 'Whatsoever thine hand findest to do, do it with all thy might.' What you are doesn't show just in the big battles, but in the little ones as well. You won't kill Goliath if you run away from a bear or a lion.

God can do so much for you if you give yourself wholly to Him and to His commands. 'Whatsoever he says unto you, do it.'

Consider Joseph. In Potiphar's home, in prison, or in charge of Egypt's harvests, he put everything he had into his job. That was the way he became master of Egypt. Do what you can, when you can, and all you can, wherever you are, and God will make you ruler over much.

When I laid my hands on Sister C, I had been shown something important. The gifts of the Spirit are not to be reserved for some future occasion, but are to be used today. With the hand of God upon you, 'Take up bow and arrow. Open the window. Shoot.'

PART FOUR

Success

13

Impotent or Important?

The sign of the living Christ is an empty tomb, not an empty church. Back-street missions are not the ideal for which Jesus died.

Some think a successful church, one that attracts all manner of people, can't be spiritual. What is our vision? God with His back to the wall? God as a charitable cause? A make-do church, always threadbare, merely scraping the bottom of the barrel?

From Genesis to Revelation, no such picture is found. God's servants went to the nations. They turned the tides of history. Paul caused Felix to tremble. He could say to the Roman Governor Festus, King Agrippa, Queen Bernice and numerous high officials, 'This thing was not done in a corner' (Acts 26:26). Jesus challenged the whole of Israel and its rulers. After He had ascended, the whole world faced the same challenge. Paul witnessed before the Emperor Nero himself.

Is your God a nonentity? Is He impotent? Or is He important and omnipotent? My God is not the God of a little ghetto of believers that nobody need take any notice of. The God to serve is the great I AM, the One who cowed Pharaoh.

The Bible is a success story. The idea of a gospel which doesn't make progress is the exact opposite to the gospel we read of in the word. The Bible sets before the church a plan for advance in the face of all opposition and evil.

We have seen plenty of opposition in the world. The Devil reigned in some areas. We came up against antagonism, false religion, crime and sin in all forms. But the gospel has battered the Devil. Multitudes beyond number have started to follow the conquering King Jesus. African governments have supported our CfaN gospel crusades, and at times have even given us official police escorts from airports and to the crusade sites.

In the next two or three chapters, I want to encourage the expectation of blessing for the work of God. Anything else would not be the word of God. The Bible never offers us comfort for decline. God's servants are committed to triumph. Pentecost is revival.

If you read the books of Exodus, Deuteronomy, Joshua, Samuel, Kings and Chronicles, you will discover the principles of success—and also those of failure. We will look to these scriptures. First we will turn to Joshua, which ought to be called 'The Book of Success', and then we will turn to the scriptures concerning David, Jonathan and Elisha.

14

Seven Steps to Success

Some have wishes. Others, like Joshua, have purposes. A whole generation of Israel wished, and died still wishing. They had a wishbone but no backbone. Joshua turned 'wishes' into land, cities, homes and possessions. Unbelieving Israel whined and died in the wilderness. Believing Joshua wined and dined in Canaan, the Promised Land.

When God said 'go', even after forty years, Joshua still had 'go'—his go had not gone. Within three days he went. Israel had given up. To them, the Promised Land was a fantasy. Joshua made the 450-year-old dream come true.

Once God had commissioned him, Joshua did not wait. The right moment had come, but then the right moment was always at once for Joshua. It was not a question of striking while the iron was hot, but of striking *until* the iron was hot. He did not wait for a special day. Joshua made the day an occasion. For forty years, Joshua had seen a victory waiting to happen. It happened when he decided. The door of history swung open at his touch.

Now, look at the seven factors behind his success, set

out in the Book of Joshua, chapter one. All the seven
victory factors lay in his own heart, not in his circumstances. That is the difference between what happens for
some people and what does not happen for others. Success
is in ourselves, not in our circumstances.

> The Lord spake unto Joshua...Moses' minister, saying,
> 'Moses my servant is dead; now therefore arise, go...' (vv 1–
> 2).

What a moment to go. It began with a funeral. The man
who was supposed to lead them was dead. 'Now go,' the
Lord instructed. If God had said, 'Moses, my servant is
dead, so you can't go now. You had better go back to
Egypt,' it could have been expected. It was a disastrous
hour. However, such a time is the hour for God. He revels
in doing things in disastrous hours, bringing life out of
death.

And Joshua! Moses was one of the half dozen greatest
men of all time, brought up as a prince, a genius, a born
leader, an organiser, a writer, a personality who carried
with him the aura of God as no other man on earth. How
could Joshua compare to this giant? Would Israel say,
'Who does this Joshua think he is? Why, he was only
Moses' servant! He—lead us?'

Moses should have led them into Canaan, but never
did, for all his mental and spiritual stature. How could
any lesser man do it? To Joshua, the answer was that he
could do what Moses did not do, because Moses had
already accomplished what Joshua could never have done.
Since Moses had been before him and done his mighty
work, Joshua now could take the land. Moses had done
everything he could. If Joshua did not take the final step
over into Canaan, he would fail Moses.

Great men have gone before us all. It would be easy to
feel too small to take their places. People ask, 'Where are
the new Pauls and Peters, the present-day Luthers and
Wesleys?' But God does not want those men today. He
wants us—the way He made us. Joshua was the man for

Canaan. Those great ones of the past made everything ready for us—for the final push before Jesus comes. We must not let them down.

Those who went before us fought for freedom, for the Bible, for truth, for the Holy Spirit. They have left us wonderful resources. We can take up where they left off. Pygmies can wave the torches of giants. Remember that even Jesus said, 'Greater works than these shall he do' (Jn 14:12).

Christian giants did their job, and now we do ours. They did not evangelise the world, but they opened it up. God says, 'Paul is dead, Livingstone is dead. Now arise, go in and possess the land.' What they could not do, we can do. The vision in their hearts is the vista before our very eyes—the world for Jesus Christ. We must cast off our feelings of inferiority. Some compare Christians today with Christians of the past. A man's greatness lies only in God in any age. Joshua could do what Moses did not— because he had Moses' God.

That is the first secret—realise your greatness is in God. 'With God all things are possible.' Note the preposition 'with', not 'to', God. To *you* all things are possible, with God.

As I said unto Moses (v 3).

What had God said? 'Every place that the sole of your foot shall tread upon, that have I given unto you.' Joshua rode into Canaan upon the promises of God. God had not said it to Moses only. He had given the land to Abraham, Isaac, Jacob and Joseph. Israel inherited the promise. But that promise was not to be fulfilled merely for the physical descendants of these great men. Only those who were the 'faith' descendants of Abraham could claim the Promised Land.

One entire generation of Abraham's physical offspring died on the wrong side of the border, in unbelief. Two men were his true children: Caleb and Joshua. The faithless all died in the wilderness—they had disinherited themselves. The two faith children lived and went in, later leading a believing second generation there. How? They took the land by stepping on it. They were not content merely with the title deeds. They entered into their estate.

That is the second secret. All of God's promises that were made to others become ours by faith. They are made-to-measure promises, tailored to our needs. They are as much for you as if God personally had appeared and spoken to you—your only requirement is to put them on. The Lord's question was, and is, 'How long are ye slack to possess the land?' Joshua said, 'There remaineth much land to be possessed.' In fact, they didn't yet own one acre. The only land remaining to be possessed was what Joshua had made up his mind to have. It was theirs by faith. 'Faith is the substance of things hoped for.' He had a vision, laid claim to it, and went ahead to get it.

> From the wilderness and this Lebanon even unto the...river Euphrates, all the land of the Hittites, and unto the great sea toward the going down of the sun, shall be your coast (v 4).

People read in the Book of Joel of dreams and visions. They want visions—for a thrill, a supernatural experience, a mystical pleasure. That is not what God intended. His visions are given to change the world. God's true dreamers are practical men, not mystics. Believing dreamers are realists. The stuff of their dreams is concrete substance.

We don't stumble on success accidentally. Joshua had an aim, a vision. Hope, one of the three great abiding Christian qualities, is created by vision. Faith makes hope feasible.

It is even better than that. Joshua's secret of success was that he was hungry for God's maximum. The boundaries described there have their own secret—they are expandable, encompassing anywhere from 135,000 to one million square kilometres. When God said 'the river Euphrates', its geographical position meant that Israel could extend to any point on the river—the border was expandable. It allowed for ever-increasing faith and ever-enlarging vision. God had given a rubberband promise with a built-in elasticity which could satisfy the spiritually boldest. Joshua's attitude was one of a man of faith.

What a dream for Israel. After all, they were runaway slaves. Joshua dreamed dreams. Dreamers are the folk who change the world. Joshua was no longer a youth, and he anticipated the prophecy of Joel—'Your old men shall dream dreams.' Dreams of world conquest for Christ are a charismatic feature. That was the very vision which drove people to seek the power of Pentecost at the beginning of the Pentecostal revival. This is what God sent the power to do.

That is the third secret of success. Get a vision of what you should do for God, then work to bring it about. Without vision, the people perish.

As I was with Moses, so I will be with thee (v 5).

It is one of the most deeply-rooted beliefs (actually, 'unbeliefs'), that God is more with some people than with others. We even make all kinds of conditions by which we explain why He is; some are more holy, or more prayerful or something. As if the presence of God depended upon *us!* The promise of His presence is unconditional. From the beginning God said 'I will never leave thee nor forsake thee'. He said it to Joshua and it is repeated 1300 years later in Hebrews (13:5). God is with us not because we are good or when we have great faith He is there. No such terms are laid down. He is with us because He has committed Himself to it, irrevocably, as it were 'for better for worse, for richer for poorer, in sickness and in health—'I Thy maker am thine Husband', He said.

To judge whether He is with people or not, we go by the wrong signs. We look at this man or that and judge him by what he accomplishes or fails to accomplish. Does God shrink or swell according to who He is with? God is not more with an evangelist than He is with a pastor, or more with a pastor than He is with a church member. He is not more with a big church than with a little assembly, or more with Moses than with Joshua.

Moses had the most extraordinary experiences with God a man ever had. Joshua could not share these experiences fully at the time. But it was to Joshua that God said, 'I will not fail thee, nor forsake thee.' The presence of God with us does not vary with our callings or with our successes. If God was only with us when we had success, success would never come.

People often say, 'Why does God use that man? I could do what he does.' Exactly—you could! So why not start now and do what the other man is doing? How can He use you if you never do what that man does? That is why He doesn't use you.

A disgruntled employee stood by his boss' desk, complaining that he earned so much less than his boss. He said, 'I could be sitting where you are. I am as good an engineer as you are.' The boss replied, 'That's right, you could be sitting here. Why aren't you? I started this business with nothing, and you could have done the same.'

That is the fourth secret of success. Go forth knowing God is with you, as much as He was with anybody. Don't hang around for the right circumstances. God is your circumstance. He is with you. Others simply took advantage of this great circumstance, believed it and acted on it. God proved it. Joshua's name was originally 'Hoshea' (salvation), but Moses added the divine name to it, making 'Jehoshua', or, in English, 'Joshua'. Your name, linked with God's name, means something. You then go forth in the name of the Lord.

Be strong and of a good courage (v 6).

Only be thou strong and very courageous (v 7).

Be strong and of a good courage; be not afraid, neither be thou dismayed (v 9).

God drummed this into the soul of Joshua three times.

After the first time He gave the first reason—'I will be with thee.' The second time He added 'only': 'Only be thou strong and courageous.' On the third repetition He gave another reason—'Have not I commanded thee?' God commands, and that is when God commends.

God gives us reasons for going forward. We can always find reasons for holding back. Then we treat our fears as virtues. We say, 'I am not one to push myself.' Or, 'If God wants me to do it, He will put me there.' Or, 'We must not run in front of God.' Or, 'I am waiting for a clear leading from God—we must not presume.' Or, 'I do not seek great things for myself, but I try to keep humble.'

Men are dying. Are these honest or sufficient reasons? Or is our fear holding us back? For everything which the Devil would throw at us to make us afraid, God has given us something to counteract it. There are indeed causes for our hesitations and nervousness. That is the natural thing. But God calls us to a new life of adventure and daring. That is the exhilaration of the Christian life. Paul said he was 'not afraid to preach the gospel at Rome'. Maybe he was nervous about it, as he was at Corinth where he said he went 'in fear and trembling'. But he did not give way to his feelings. He enjoyed the experience of God strengthening him as he faced pagan Europe nearly single-handedly.

Turn to a few scriptures about fear, and see how to handle it.

'What time I am afraid, I will trust on thee' (Ps 56:3).

'The righteous are bold as a lion' (Prov 28:1).

'He spake boldly in the name of the Lord' (Acts 9:29).

'Paul and Barnabas...speaking boldly in the Lord' (Acts 14:3).

'He began to speak boldly in the synagogue' (Acts 18:26).

'He...spake boldly for the space of three months' (Acts 19:8).

'...they saw the boldness of Peter and John' (Acts 4:13).

'Lord...grant unto thy servants, that with all boldness they may speak thy word' (Acts 4:29).

'They spake the Word of God with great boldness' (Acts 4:31).

These men were not super-humans who didn't know what fear was. They felt its quivering pangs. So did Elijah, whom James said was subject to like passions as ourselves. They conquered their fears, however. How? They remembered God had sent them. They obeyed and threw the responsibility to Him. 'Have not I commanded thee?' rang in their ears. In that case, why fear man, 'whose breath is in his nostrils'?

Paul never asked people to pray for him that the power of the Spirit would rest upon him. He knew it already did (Rom 15:29). God was with him. He requested only 'that utterance may be given unto me, that I may open my mouth boldly, to make known the mystery of the gospel, for which I am an ambassador in bonds: that therein I may speak boldly, as I ought to speak' (Eph 6:19–20). Note the 'as I ought to speak', for he was God's ambassador sent to speak.

There is the fifth secret of success: boldness in Christ. Wesley said, 'I am too afraid of God to be afraid of men.' The fear of God casts out the fear of man. Jesus said, 'Be not afraid, only believe' (Mk 5:36); literally, 'Don't have phobia, have faith.' The opposite of fear is not courage, but faith.

> Observe to do according to all the law, which Moses my servant commanded thee: turn not from it to the right hand or to the left, that thou mayest prosper whithersoever thou goest. This book of the law shall not depart out of thy mouth; but thou shalt meditate therein day and night, that thou mayest observe to do according to all that is written therein: for then thou shalt make thy way prosperous, and then thou shalt have good success (v 8).

That word contains every secret. You might read the most erudite books about the Bible. Scholarship is excellent, but 'the secret of the Lord is with them that fear him'. The hidden things of God—these are not known by the intellect. They are incommunicable. They rise and flower in our souls as we read the word. The Bible is not a book of cryptic mysteries. It is plain enough, but only grasped by the hand of faith.

When Christ taught us to pray, 'Give us this day our daily bread,' he also meant the word of God. Read it daily. The Father will then interpret it to us and feed our souls daily. The Bible is not for pedantics. Some want to correct others about phrases and words, but miss the throb of God's heart.

A preacher has one task: the word, as Paul said to Titus. Preach the word, meditate in the word at all times ('day and night'), get your message from the word. Say what it says. Never be selective, adjusting the gospel to suit the public palate.

'Here may the wretched sons of want exhaustless riches find.' You will never be short of ministry as long as you are full of the word. Read it when you cannot study it. It is not the 'deep things', dug up by going through a whole reference library, but the simplest statement which can set you on fire—and ignite others as well. Throughout the world, the need for word ministry is only too apparent. Preachers with stories, jokes, 'thoughts', psychology, charming speeches and good advice are aplenty. Some have nothing to offer except a neat homiletical arrangement, nicely illiterated with correct introduction and denouement, like a beautiful frame with no picture.

The word makes a man a prophet, not a mere pulpit performer. Understanding of the word is vital. Any man who gives himself to teaching and preaching this word will find multitudes of hungry people waiting, like fledglings in a nest.

Most of all, the power of God is released through the gospel which is the word of God (1 Pet 1:25). Every time it is being preached, it creates. It is a wonderful moment when the Holy Spirit acts, as He is bound to act. There is no need to prove Scripture. It will prove itself.

That is the sixth secret of success. 'This book of the law shall not depart from thy mouth.' If others are prosperous without it, do not follow them. For you, here is the real way—the word, THE word, THE WORD.

> Within three days ye shall pass over this Jordan, to go in to possess the land, which the Lord your God giveth you to possess it (v 11).

This is what I like about Joshua—he was immediate. Israel had been on the east bank of the Jordan for an entire generation. That river was not very wide, but it may as well have been the ocean. The other side was only a legend of their fathers, a cloud nine golden fancy, the beautiful isle of somewhere and sometime.

Then, Moses dead, one morning like any other, when it looked as if they would be tent-dwellers in the wilderness for ever, the trumpet sounded. The people were galvanised. The gates of history swung open. 'Prepare to enter the land in three days.'

How many Christian dreams and ideas have been shelved, put aside as idealistic, for some indefinite future? God has no indefinite futures. He gives commands and promises for immediate realisation. The Father knows the hour. The Revival everybody wants—now. Signs and wonders—now. Bold going forth with the gospel—now. Opening those new churches—now.

They crossed Jordan and looked at the key city, Jericho. As the faithless spies had said, 'Walled up to heaven, and we are as grasshoppers.' That grasshopper mentality! 'As [a man] thinketh in his heart, so is he' (Prov 23:7). If you think you are a grasshopper, you are. A man is what he believes. You are not a grasshopper in God—never.

God included dwarfs among those who 'shall not approach to offer the bread of his God' (Lev 21:17–20). The only dwarfs in God's sight are people little in faith, suffering from a grasshopper-syndrome. The 'full stature of the man' does not see himself as a grasshopper who is unable to take the Promised Land.

The walls were there, dwarfing all of them, like the ten faithless spies had reported long before. But now Israel was inspired. They felt big enough to blow those walls down with the blast of a trumpet—they needed no dynamite. And blow them down they did. They walked around the walls for six days, with Jericho's inhabitants jeering, amused by such odd warfare. Then, down the walls went. We are big, but only in God.

There is the seventh secret of success. Go in now to take the land. Israel did not just march and blow trumpets. When the walls fell, they went in, fought and took the city. Long ago the walls of the city fell when, as Jesus said, He saw Satan fall as lightning from heaven. 'Now is the prince of this world cast out,' but that is not all that has to be done. We now go in over those fallen walls with the sword of the word to preach the gospel and to take the city for God.

15

Positive Initiative

'Find your gift and use it,' the experts say. If you have a gift, take that advice. Don't bury your talent in the earth. But...this advice could be an excuse for some folk to settle back in their armchairs. They will profess that they have no gift.

The Bible has a better way. 'Whatsoever thine hand findeth to do, do it with thy might' (Eccles 9:12). Get into God's vineyard, even if you only do a bit of weeding.

See what has to be done, and get on with it. In some cases, the call of God is the need. If you look at whether you are gifted for a task or not, you might decide it doesn't lie within your province. You may leave it to someone else. It is the call of God and what needs to be done that matters.

We need not consult with ourselves about our gifts, for by faith God can lift us beyond ourselves and our limitations. It isn't you who does the work. It's God. Without Him, you can do nothing. You can do all things through Christ. We can walk on the water if need be, for all things are possible to him that believeth.

Faith in God makes the man. What we believe, we are—even when we don't believe we are anything. Don't undersell yourself to yourself. Selling yourself short is not humility, but a denial of the very purpose for which you were born. Here is a vital principle: the call of God must be obeyed if you want the power of God to work through you.

What does God want you to do? The first thing He wants you to do, is *not* to spend years finding out what He wants. God keeps no one waiting for that long. If He wants a job done, there would be no point in keeping us guessing about it. Why should He do that? It would be ridiculous to hide from you what His wishes for you are. Nor will He make it terribly difficult for you to find out.

He always has a task at hand. It may not be a great task, it may be nothing heroic. Perhaps it is a job almost beneath your dignity, even one that could be considered menial. Paul sat making tents—not planning intents. Faithful in the little, God made him master of much.

Some are asking God to speak to them and guide them because they despise the day of small beginnings. They assume God has some great work for them and that it surely cannot be a little thing. 'Seekest thou great things for thyself? Seek them not,' said Jeremiah to his secretary/servant (Jeremiah 45:5). You can't steer a boat that isn't moving. God waits for you to move before He tells you which direction to take. God does guide. 'I being in the way, the Lord led me....' You take the initiative for God. That is how Paul went on those famous travels.

Action

If there is a hole in the dam, plug it. Don't pass a resolution about it. If a foe is breaking into the Promised Land, the demand is obvious. Fight! Don't wait! Don't ask God what to do, or study whether you have the gift. One man who either did not wait when he should, or did wait when he shouldn't, was King Saul. Doing nothing because we can't do something mighty is nothing but pride. But we have another lesson now.

The worst of times is the best of times

For centuries, there was competition between Israel and the Philistines for the land of Israel. The Philistines were the traditional enemies to Israel, both physically and spiritually. We can compare spiritual principles in that history to Christian work and warfare today. Constant Israeli-Philistine skirmishes took place, until David finally subdued the Philistines.

After Saul became King, he created a standing army of 3,000 men, placing a third of them under his son Jonathan. At that time, the Philistines had the upper hand. They put garrisons here and there throughout the land of Israel, including one in the strategic pass from Bethel to Jericho, where the town of Michmash stood.

Jonathan had already made an attack on the Philistine forces at this time, so the Philistines had placed a good army in Michmash. In readiness, King Saul placed about 600 men on the other side of the pass, at Gibea. He was all set for war.

But Saul only waited. His finger was on the trigger, but he didn't pull it. The enemy sat there comfortably in Israel, occupying and exploiting the good land. It was a phony war. Nobody did anything. The Philistines didn't need to do anything, but Israel should have done something.

Now Jonathan was like David. They were soul mates with a similar, restless temperament of do or die. Jonathan became impatient just sitting there, fingering the blades of grass, one elbow on the ground. He thought of his father who 'tarried under a pomegranate tree', keeping cool.

Eventually, saying nothing to his father, Jonathan and his armour bearer decided to take action themselves, just the two of them. The enemy was there, so why leave them unmolested? They would settle down in the land for ever if something wasn't done.

Two daring disciples

Now the passage to the small Philistine garrison above them led through a defile, which at one point passed between two sharp rocks. Jonathan would not only have to climb up, which gave the defenders an advantage against him, he would also have to get through that narrow defensive position. One Philistine could hold off an army there, like Horatius did at the Tiber bridge. So Jonathan said to his shield bearer, 'It may be that the Lord will work for us: for there is no restraint to the Lord to save by many or by few.'

It was a venture of faith. They knew the Lord could save by the two of them. However, the Lord couldn't save at all if everybody kept cool under pomegranate trees. Such inaction would allow the occupying enemy to sit pretty for ever. Some Israeli action was needed. It didn't matter to God whether it was done officially or by personal initiative.

So they decided on a test. They would come out of hiding and stand where the Philistines could see them. Then, if their enemies said, 'Come up here and we'll show you a thing or two' (1 Sam 14:12), Jonathan and his armour bearer would do just that. The Philistines never would have believed that they would attempt such a foolhardy escapade, two against twenty, an army close by, and the twenty soldiers in the commanding position above them.

Notice what Jonathan's test was. In it was an act of faith. He proposed to do something very courageous, and his 'fleece' was that the Philistines would challenge him if he made himself conspicuous, something his enemies certainly would do. Some people put out 'fleeces' which are absurd, and take guidance from conditions which are either too easy or too hard. These are those who usually get fleeced by the Devil in the end.

The Philistines did see Jonathan, and said exactly what we might expect: 'Come up here.' They, too, were not spoiling for battle at the time. They never believed the two young Israeli soldiers would attempt to go up. So they turned their backs and carried on, doing nothing in particular.

But, in faith, Jonathan and his armour bearer did what was considered venturesome to attempt. The pair of them went up, creeping forward on hands and knees. They sprang an attack on the astonished garrison and caught them unprepared. Jonathan's faith gave him a sheer audacity which won the day.

Meanwhile, what was Saul doing? He was found talking to a priest of the Lord, probably seeking help and guidance, when it was obvious what his duty was. He hoped God would do something (1 Sam 14:3). God would do something—as soon as somebody would believe Him and go into action.

God, in fact, did do something—when Jonathan went into action. The daring attack came off. To begin with, the Lord helped their valour. Then He rose in His might and did His own thing. He brought about an earth tremor, not uncommon perhaps in that area.

The outcome was panic. It spread throughout the enemy lines. The Philistine force became confused, rumours gathered. They began to flee. Jonathan's father, King Saul, heard the commotion. He found courage and led his men into the mêlée, giving chase. Even the prisoners whom the Philistines were holding took heart and turned on their captors. The Israeli people who had hidden themselves among the rocks of Mount Ephraim, too frightened before to fight, now became bold and threw their weight into the route of the enemy. Trapped, the Philistines' cause suffered a severe setback.

Ordinary day

Notice when this happened. 'Now it came to pass upon a day.' Well, it had to happen 'on a day'—some day or another! This phrase means that it was no special day. It was a day without divine leadings and revelations. The victory occurred because Jonathan made up his mind to fight. He made that day special himself. God's day coincided exactly with the day when Jonathan decided that they had hung around long enough. It always does. It was an unpromising day without auspicious signs. There were not particularly good conditions—the conditions were bad, in fact, and no different from when the Philistines had penetrated the land earlier.

The King had been waiting for something to happen, perhaps waiting to be pushed into action. He wanted a divine leading or hoped God would make the first move, which was why he talked to the priest. Jonathan couldn't hang around for eventualities and signs. He consulted no priest. His 'fleece', testing God's will, was almost sure to put him into battle. No wonder Jonathan was a man after David's heart and, remember, David was a man after God's heart.

God has a thousand-year calendar with only one day on it. It is marked 'today'. Jesus Himself challenged those who talked about 'waiting for harvest in four months', and said, 'The harvest is ripe now.' The Prophet Haggai launched a blistering attack on people in Jerusalem once when they said, 'The time is not come, the time that the Lord's house should be built' (Hagg 1:2). It was not time to build God's house, but they built their own houses nonetheless.

Revival initiative

Too often people say that the time isn't right. As if weather or circumstances could thwart the power of God. Revival isn't for when there *is* revival, but for when there isn't a sign of it. Revivals always begin when nothing is happening, when there are no signs of God's moving and nothing encouraging on the horizon. Precisely *because* things were bad all around, bold men of faith went out to change them. If we wait until the situation is better, we shall never go at all. In fact, what's the point then? Jonathan struck when a victory was impossible, and that is why he succeeded. God delighted to join in and prove His power.

We are all praying for a mighty revival to sweep Europe and the rest of the world. Pray, pray on! But don't wait until it comes and gospel preaching then becomes easy. Get on with what you can do now. You can win thousands for Christ while waiting for revival. And not only that, such action could be the start of revival. It is true that revival is 'a sovereign act of God', as many believe. But it is equally true that revival can be caused. The early Christians certainly knew this, because Mark 16:20 declares: 'And they went forth, and preached every where, the Lord working with them, and confirming the word with signs following. Amen.'

Those blessed people didn't sit and wait for the Lord to go forth, as so many do today. 'And *they* went forth....' In other words, they took the initiative and the Lord gladly obliged. I am fully persuaded that God allows us to pull the trigger for mighty outpourings of His Holy Spirit. By His grace, I have witnessed it numerous times. We need Holy Ghost initiative. Revival takes anointed men and women of God who exercise the audacity of faith.

When Jonathan and his armour bearer went up by their own initiative for a private skirmish with the enemy on their hands and knees, they wrought a far bigger victory than they thought possible. Is God waiting for you? Are you His Jonathan?

Anybody can believe God when God is already moving. Real faith acts when God doesn't seem to be acting. God loves the man and woman who gamble upon His help. This is the formula for triumph, blessing and revival.

How many more people can you think of who did

exactly that? Think of anybody who achieved new things for God, and you can put every one of them on this list. Every one was somebody who dared when nobody else thought it was the time. Every revival has started that way.

One minister longed for God's greater movings, to see the Lord heal the afflicted and work miracles. When he approached an older minister, he was told, 'God will do those things when revival comes. So wait.' It was like that when Jesus was in Nazareth, too. The unfriendly congregation put off indefinitely what God promised He would do, like most in the land did. But Jesus declared, 'This Scripture is this day fulfilled in your ears'—in a town like Nazareth at that, with its bad reputation.

How much revival atmosphere could there be in a synagogue where a man was there with a withered hand, and all the cynics were watching, hoping to accuse Jesus of healing on the Sabbath? The conditions were hardly propitious. But Jesus healed the man—because the time is ripe when the need is greatest.

That time, I am sure, is today. Who is God waiting for? Could it be you? What are *you* waiting for?

16

No Bargains with the Devil

The white horse

From time to time, I have been invited to join a television panel to discuss religious issues. The participants generally meet just before going on the air. On one occasion, none of us knew each other, and we had to be introduced. There was a short time in which to chat with one another before the programme began. Conversation got around to horse racing, as it was the time of the July Handicap. One of the men, who professed to be an atheist, seemed to have the names of all the horses and jockeys at his fingertips. I couldn't say anything, as I had no knowledge of horse racing and betting. So, I had to sit quietly, just occupying the time with silent prayer. I wanted the Lord to guide me in the discussion that soon would take place. The others continued to discuss horses and gambling, and then, suddenly, something flashed through my spirit. It roused me, and I turned to the expert. 'Now I want to tell you something about horses,' I said. The atheist was interested. I said, 'I have put all my money on the white horse in the Book of Revelation.' Perhaps he thought that I was an authority and had just been silent on the subject. He looked baffled and repeated, 'White horse, in the Book of Revelation?' That seemed to be the only horse that particular expert didn't know about. 'Well, tell me, who's the rider on the white horse?' he asked. Inside, I felt glad, for his question was exactly the one I had wanted. He expected me to say who the jockey was. For me, it was exciting to tell him. 'In Revelation, chapter 19, it says that the rider's name is "Faithful and True, The Word of God," the Son of God, Jesus Christ, and,' I went on, 'Mister, I have not put just my money on Him. As a matter of fact, I have no money. I have put my life and my soul on Him. He's the One I back with everything I've got, and I know I am going to win.'

That is where the race starts for us: with the finish 'a dead cert', in racing terms. For us, the end is a living certainty. It is the assurance of Jesus as the eternal and universal Winner. Knowledge like that is bound to have a tremendous effect upon our everyday lives.

The uncurseable winner

Do you know, with absolute assurance, that you have joined the winning side? Then you will not be harassed by fear. There is no way a believer can be crushed. He is uncurseable. He has the Winner, God Himself, on his side. 'If God be for us, who can be against us?' (Rom 8:31).

Fear is forged in hell. It is issued by Satan as a standard weapon to all demons. They know the meaning of fear. It has a paralysing force. Demons are full of fear themselves, like scorpions are full of poison. Fear is Satan's venom. He wants to sting us all, making us sick with fear. The Devil will create a future for us packed with fears. But they are illusions—fears are mere phantoms. They will only take on substance if we accept them. We must exorcise these ghosts.

Fear is the first thing to be rid of. The Evil One will

surround evangelism with a cloud of misgiving. Conquering dread is the blow against the Enemy which neutralises his primary attack. 'No weapon that is formed against thee shall prosper' (Is 54:17). We have our own weapon, the word of God, the sword of the Spirit, that is the word in the hand of the Spirit (Eph 6:17). Know the word, learning from it that we are not at the mercy of Satan.

We can look at an example, the story of Balak's plot to curse Israel (Num 22–24). Israel had been undefeated on the battlefield. Balak, therefore, resorted to other means. He offered Balaam money to curse Israel. Balaam was not unwilling. He loved money. He knew the Lord did not want to curse Israel, but he asked anyway, just in case, obviously to get the reward. He sought the Lord, hoping God would give him that kind of prophecy.

Balak and Balaam clambered to the rocky peaks of the 'high places of Baal', building seven altars and offering seven bulls and rams in sacrifice as well. Perhaps some dark, occultic force might have obliged Balaam and Balak, blighting the progress of God's people. But God does not deal in curses against His own people. Balaam and Balak persisted, however, trying hard from every angle. They found the attempt was futile.

Balak and Balaam looked at the tents of Israel at the foot of the high hills. In the midst of the camp was the Tabernacle, with the glory of God's presence, the very banner of the Lord, constantly there. 'He that keepeth Israel shall neither slumber nor sleep' (Ps 121:4). Israel was resting there early in the morning, safe beneath the outspread wings of Jehovah, which were invisible to Israel's enemies.

Balaam and Balak did their worst on the top of the mountain. Raging, they worked to cast a spell of misfortune over the Israelites. But God's people slept on peacefully. Balaam opened his mouth to curse, but his words came forth as blessings instead. The tribes were there, all the time unaware and undisturbed. The Israelites were relaxing their heads on the pillow of His promises. They were safe under His divine protection.

The attempt to turn dark forces against Israel only succeeded in making the two plotters look ridiculous. I like the way the Bible concludes the episode. It has a touch of quiet mockery. 'And Balaam rose up, and went and returned to his place: and Balak also went his way' (Num 24:25). That's all that happened.

Now look at what Balaam had to say in Numbers 23:8, 21: 'How shall I curse, whom God hath not cursed? or how shall I defy, whom the Lord hath not defied? The Lord his God is with him, and the shout of a king is among them.'

Frightening Satan

Fear plays into the hands of the Devil. He can do no real damage, except to make us fear that he can. The Devil is a con artist. Balaam was forced to speak the truth. He wound up showing us that God's people are not for cursing. We are immune. We are redeemed, as were Israel. What was true of God's redeemed people then, is true of the redeemed today. Fear hears the shout of Goliath, but faith hears the shout of the King of kings.

'There is no enchantment against Jacob, neither is there any divination against Israel...it shall be said of Jacob and of Israel, What hath God wrought!' (Num 23:23).

The howling winds of death had been heard across Egypt not long before. Yet no Israeli home knew its cold breath. The blood of the lamb of the passover marked every household. Jehovah, on hovering wings, protected them from the avenging angel. Every child of God today is covered and marked by the blood of Jesus. Each one of us is beyond the reach of the powers of hell, of witches, of spells, of curses, of demons or of all the Devil's minions. Principalities and powers in heavenly places cannot touch us while we rest beneath the banner of the precious blood of the Saviour, our Passover Lamb. That protection is impenetrable and invulnerable. 'Ye fearful saints, fresh courage take!' The man who fears is the Devil's ally— whether he likes it or not. Fear is an infection, a sickness. It can spread among Christians. I am sure that God prohibited the children of Israel from talking while marching around the walls of Jericho because they would have spread doubt and fear among themselves. The Devil does not fear the man who fears. He knows that person is harmless. But Satan trembles when we do not fear.

Nehemiah was restoring Jerusalem. Some urged him to hide from the threats of his enemies. I like his reply: 'Should such a man as I flee? and who is there, that, being as I am, would?' (Neh 6:11). Are the people of God, the blood-bought sons and daughters of the kingdom such people as we are, to give way to bluster and threats? God's people are not given 'the spirit of fear; but of power, and of love, and of a sound mind' (2 Tim 1:7). Should such as we are flee? Never.

Far from fearing, we can rejoice. 'Behold, I give unto you power to tread on serpents and scorpions, and over all the power of the enemy; and nothing shall by any means hurt you' (Lk 10:19). Christians are not the hunted, but the hunters; not the attacked, but the attackers. We are not besieged. We do not have our backs to the wall. Far from it. We are God's storm-troops, sent to release the hostages of hell. We are the invading forces of the Lord.

Jesus again and again said, 'Fear not!' But that was not all. He was the supreme Psychologist. Notice what He said: 'Fear not, only believe.' It was always more than just, 'Don't be afraid,' or, 'Take courage, be brave.' That alone would be useless advice. Fear is a force and must be met by an equal force.

Fear is the negative force. Its sign is a minus. Somebody once said to me, 'Fear is the darkroom in which people develop their negatives.' Only a positive force can cancel a negative one. That positive force is faith. So Jesus always said, 'Fear not, only believe.' The opposite of fear is not courage, but faith.

'This is the victory that overcometh the world, even our faith' (1 Jn 5:4). Faith is a multi-purpose weapon. It is not presumption or bravado—remember the sons of Sceva. A trembling saint makes a triumphant Satan, but faith frightens the foe. We are not called to tremble, but to exercise authority and to shake hell. 'Benaiah...plucked the spear out of the Egyptian's hand and slew him with his own spear' (2 Sam 23:21). So we will snatch fear from the hands of the Enemy, use his own weapon and make devils tremble.

Prince of the power of the air

During one of our gospel crusades in Africa, I had an experience which gave me a revelation. We were to use our big tent in Green Valley. With great anticipation, I counted the hours to the first meeting, until the tent manager phoned.

They were ready to pitch the canvas tabernacle which would hold 10,000 people, African style, but he said, 'The ground is too soft. In wind and rain the anchors and masts would lose their grip, and the tent would collapse. Wet soil could not support it.' Should he go ahead and pitch it or not? My mind was working fast on this question. It would be a terrible thing if it all went wrong. I just prayed to the Lord in my heart while I thought. Then a wonderful, divine assurance flooded my mind. 'Go ahead,' I replied. 'In the name of Jesus, it is not going to rain or storm.' And so, on that instruction, the tent went up.

We had a wonderful start. Night after night the tent was packed with people hungry for the word of God. Until one afternoon, while I was kneeling in prayer in my car-avan parked near the tent. I looked up and saw a mighty thunderstorm filling the western sky, heading in our direc-tion. Have you ever seen an African storm which fills the air with water?

The clouds, like masses of pitch-black curly hair, were being tossed by the storm within them. 'Here comes your

catastrophe,' something said inside me. But then I heard
the voice of the Holy Spirit answering that fear, telling me
what to do: 'Go and rebuke the Devil!' I went out and
walked aggressively in the direction of the imminent
storm. Lifting my finger and pointing, I said, 'Devil, I
want to talk to you in the name of Jesus. If you destroy this
tent of mine, I am going to trust God for a tent three times
this size.'

I looked, and at that moment something incredible
happened—the clouds parted. They began to make a
detour away from and around the tent. The menace was
over. The clouds and rain never reached us, and the tent
stood firm for the rest of the gospel campaign. 'How great
is our God!'

Then this wonderful truth hit me, harder than any
thunderbolt which that storm may have hurled at us.
Faith frightens Satan. My faith had scared off the Devil.
He probably had enough to worry about already with this
tent of ours, and faith for a bigger one shook him.

'Devils...tremble' (Jas 2:19) the Bible declares. When
we arise with living faith and tackle the opposition in
God's strength, our faith terrorises the arch-terrorist, the
Devil. 'Resist the devil, and he will flee from you' (Jas 4:7)
the word states. The Bible also instructs us to resist Satan:
'Whom resist stedfast in the faith' (1 Pet 5:9). This is no
mere untried hypothesis. John could testify, 'I write unto
you, young men, because ye have overcome the wicked
one' (1 Jn 2:13). With faith in God, even 'the lame take the
prey' (Is 33:23).

My tent episode was not quite over, for something
unsettling nagged at my heart. 'What if the Devil misunderstood my words?' I wondered. The thought kept coming back to me. So I decided to make the issue clear. I
spoke to the Devil in the name of Jesus once more, telling
him, 'I make no bargains with you. Just because you
withdrew the wind and the rain this does not mean I made
an agreement with you about not having a bigger tent.
The bigger tent comes anyway.' We are not to negotiate

with the Devil—we are to cast him out. That is all the word of God tells us. Keep repeating to yourself, over and over if you must, 'Faith frightens Satan, faith frightens Satan, faith frightens Satan.' This truth will change you from negative to positive. In Jesus, you are the victor, not the victim. Satan is the victim, because Jesus crushed the serpent's head.

The fearless Christian

God's children can be bold. Let the word tell you so. 'By faith Moses, when he was born, was hid three months of his parents, because they saw he was a proper child; and they were not afraid of the king's commandment' (Heb 11:23). Just think of what that involved. The Egyptian state and Pharaoh, its head, had made it illegal to keep a male Hebrew baby. By law, such children were to be killed at birth. Soldiers moved around to carry out this order. What terror and grief there must have been.

Then Moses was born. His parents looked upon this lovely son, and they knew they could not, and never would, kill him. They decided to defy the law and hide the baby. 'By faith...they were not afraid.' Officers of the law were around, and their footsteps were heard stopping at their very door, seeking the child's life. Who would not shake in their shoes if armed men were waiting, ordered to kill their baby? Yet 'they were not afraid'. Why not? Were they unnatural, unfeeling? No, they were very good parents. There was just one reason why they did not quiver or panic—they had faith in God. True, the situation was impossible. Their faith looked naive and foolish. But the situation was exactly what God likes. He delights to do the impossible.

When things are impossible, faith is the answer. Faith is not just for the possible—that is not faith at all. The mightiest resource in the universe is the arm of God. Some can only believe God when it is for something 'reasonable', something which can be managed. But, as Paul wrote, 'We...have no confidence in the flesh' (Phil 3:3), that is, in our own schemes.

Let me tell you the African story of the elephant and the ant. An elephant crossed a shaky bridge, and a tiny ant sat on the elephant, just behind the huge animal's ear. The bridge shook as they crossed, and when they were safely on the other side, the ant said to the elephant, 'My word! We made that bridge swing all right, didn't *we?*'

This is the relationship we have with God when we rest on Him. He carries us (Is 46:4). He makes the bridge swing. He puts His weight behind us and on our side. He builds our home, our church, our business. The Lord leads us to success. In Him, we find the impossible possible.

The watershed

Faith makes the difference. It is the most basic distinction between one person and another. The entire world stands on one side or the other of the line of faith. There are only really two different types of people—not rich and poor, not black and white, not the learned and the unlearned, not Jew and Greek, not male and female. None of these distinctions really exist in Christ. God sees only believer and unbeliever. 'He that believeth...shall be saved; but he that believeth not shall be damned' (Mk 16:16).

Faith is of the new order. Unbelief is of the old and dying order. Faith is the dividing line which runs right through mankind. Having faith, or having no faith at all are the alternatives for our approach to life.

Fear sees just what man sees. Faith sees what God sees—and acts upon it. Faith creates action, and people of action, like Caleb and Joshua. Unbelief keeps us tied down in a spiritual wilderness—like Israel was for so many years. Fear and doubt magnify the difficulties, making us think people cannot be won for Christ and that the world is too strong. Without faith, we fear failure and mockery. Faith says people can be won, and so the joy of expectation grips us instead. By faith we move from minimum to maximum.

The man who lived tomorrow

There were two mummification processes widely used in Egypt. Nearly all the dead were preserved. The mighty Pharaohs were entombed in massive mausoleums, multiple coffins, and sometimes even under permanent pyramids. Those dead people were very dead. But one of them had no intention of having 'R.I.P.' (rest in peace) on his grave in Egypt. The mummy of Joseph was intended for export—the only one that ever was. Joseph knew the promises of God and what the future would hold, and he was determined not to be left out of it. Joseph, who died at the age of 110, wouldn't even be found dead in Egypt. He was the man who lived tomorrow.

'By faith Joseph...gave commandment concerning his bones' (Heb 11:22). He didn't want to lie quietly in the grave when the Red Sea and the River Jordan opened. His eye of faith saw the faithfulness of God fulfilling His word, that word which He had given to Abraham, Isaac and Jacob long before. In fact hundreds of years before it happened, Joseph shouted with the armies of men who, yet to be born, would bring down the walls of Jericho. Faith renews our youth. A man of faith, at the age of 110 years, is younger than a critical teenager. So many of our young are 'old' and futureless. They are the defeated rabble whose song is that of the Beatles: 'Yesterday, all my troubles seemed so far away...I believe in yesterday.' Without God and without hope. Where are the men of Joseph's batallion today?

God would go into action one day, and Joseph determined not to be left out of it, dead or alive. Faith gives life to the dead. It gives life to the fearful. Faith mocks at that king of terrors, death, and terrifies he who has the power of death, even the Devil. 'O death, where is thy sting?' (1 Cor 15:55).

PART FIVE

In Practice

17

The Trap

God blesses his own plans

God underwrites His own schemes. He will supply, but we must know what His supplies are for. Cash is for the Lord's business. All we need to know is what He plans to do. Find out what God is engaged in, and throw your lot in with Him. Join the firm! Then we are authorised to requisition by faith what we need from His vast stores. We can ask God to provide for what we are doing, as long as we are doing what He does.

What is He doing? He is the Saviour, the God of salvation. 'I, even I, am the Lord, and beside me there is no Saviour.' Salvation is not just an evangelist's pet subject, it is the Lord's 'great work'. God specialises in salvation. As medicine to a doctor, as music to a musician, so is the work of salvation to God. Jesus came 'to seek and to save that which was lost', and 'to bring many sons into glory'.

We are invited to work with Him, not on our own. The gospel is God's business from start to finish—His monopoly, if you like. We can't set up gospel shops for our own brand. Jesus Christ is the head of all the salvation work in the world. We can labour in company with Him, and it must be done at all costs. He will meet those costs.

A friend of mine said, 'If God is not the engine, I don't even want to give a push.' Then I added, 'But if God is the engine, I don't mind being the back light.' Move with God, and nothing can stop you. Nothing can go wrong with His plans. They don't fail or derail. What God wants to live, cannot and will not die.

In some cases, church projects are surviving only under intensive care. They have little to do with God's plans. His life is not in them. Switch off the life-support machine. If real life is there, the programmes will not need heart and lung equipment. What God wants to die, let die, and do not give artificial respiration. 'Let the dead bury the dead.' Why maintain unproductive church machinery and expect God to meet the bills? He won't. The real business of the church is winning people for Christ.

Wrongfully and rightfully careful

When it comes to evangelism I've heard people say, 'We must be careful with God's money,' as if He were a bit short of cash. It might be a sincere argument, but it looks suspiciously mean. Why hoard God's money in the bank? A church may save its money in case of an emergency, in order to have something for a rainy day. But God will look after any necessity that comes. The most specific and urgent of emergencies already has come—the need to save the dying world.

When was God 'careful', calculating every penny? Was He 'careful' when He made the trillions of stars and planets where not a soul lives? Was He 'careful' when He sent His own Son? He stripped heaven of its wealth and parted with its greatest treasure, the Only Begotten. He beggared Himself of all He loved and all He had for the salvation of our souls. 'If God spared not his own Son, but delivered him up for us all, how shall he not with him freely give us all things?' We have an extravagant God!

God's money plan

The Lord fills our pockets for soul-saving. When we empty them, there will be more. God's money plan is simple. 'Give, and it shall be given unto you.' Give then you will have more to give more. God spares neither Himself nor the money to find lost men and women. A church can't afford to save money instead of saving souls. Spend to save! But spend it on soul-winning projects. People will give to a live project, but not to a dead bank account. When the collection takes longer than the preaching, something is wrong. The evangelism report should come before the treasurer's report. The truth is, evangelism does not appear on the agenda at all in thousands of church business sessions. The bank statement produces more discussion than the conversion figures for the month.

The church that gives, prospers. Evangelism and support of missions is essential for the health of a church. That has been proven too often to be doubted.

Tents and intents

God guides then provides. He leads then feeds. That is His rule. An illustration is found with Israel. In the wilderness, manna fell where the pillar of cloud and fire was— and there only. If Israel missed God's leading pillar, they missed breakfast, lunch and dinner. There is always enough if we are in the spot where He tells us to be.

When we were building our 34,000-seater tent in Africa, we were in dire need of finances. The Lord had told me not to take out a bank loan, and His instructions are holy to me. Ringing in my ears were the words, 'Mine are the silver and gold.' Then one day, a very large sum indeed arrived, just what we needed, in fact. I could hardly believe my eyes, but not because my faith was small. It was because of where the gift had come from. The donor was a lady who in the past had sent us a couple of dollars a month. Then suddenly she mailed this large gift.

This was something I felt I had to know about. I visited her to find out what had prompted her to send this amount. What she told me was too exciting to put into words. She said that in the middle of the night she had had a telephone call. The voice had given her an instruction to send this particular amount of money to us. 'But,' she insisted, 'the call was not from a human being. It was an angel of the Lord who spoke to me. I know because the glory of the Lord filled my room. I knew that God had given me a clear instruction. So I did just what He told me.'

Well, I thought, if God has put an angel in charge of our finances, I need have no sleepless nights. I can sleep the sleep of the just and relax, as long as I am in partnership with Him.

Donkeys

Let me say that although the Lord told me not to take out a bank loan then, that does not mean that bank loans are wrong. We should not condemn those who are led differently from ourselves. God provided manna from the skies, but He has other ways, also. Jesus Himself used different methods. Let us look at one of them. When Jesus prepared for His triumphal entry into Jerusalem, he needed an animal to ride upon. This is what happened:

> Ascending up to Jerusalem...when he was come nigh to...the mount of Olives, he sent two of his disciples, saying, 'Go ye into the village over against you; in the which at your entering ye shall find a colt tied, whereon yet never man sat: loose him, and bring him hither. And if any man ask you, Why do ye loose him? thus shall ye say unto him, Because the Lord hath need of him' (Lk 19:28–31).

Matthew 21:2 supplements that Jesus also had a colt with the donkey. Jesus did not call a prayer meeting to pray to get these animals, then wait for somebody to bring them. In this case He took the initiative. 'Go ye into the village...loose him, and bring him...the Lord hath need of him.' The Lord was the One who had created all the donkeys there were. Why did He have to ask for one? It tells me that the Lord has needs which He gives us the privilege of fulfilling. 'The Lord hath need....'

His work has needs which you, I and all God's children can supply. It is God's wonderful arrangement to give us the joy of sharing with Him in what He does. This ought to make us happy. I imagine that later the owner of the donkeys, after he understood, must have thanked the Lord all his life for this privilege. Even the little donkey had his day. He had helped Jesus a mile or two along His way to triumph.

I noticed that the man had 'securely tightened' his donkey. It was his, and he didn't want to lose it. The Lord said to His disciples, 'Loose it!' Let's untie our donkeys for Jesus. Jesus always taught that we should not hold tightly to our money. We should loose our donkeys now, or we may lose them in the end.

> We lose what on ourselves we spend,
> We have as treasure without end
> Whatever Lord to Thee we lend.
> Who givest all.

It is biblical to take up offerings to do what God wants done. God loves a cheerful giver, because He is one Himself. Nobody can evangelise the world alone. We all have gifts to contribute: money, talents, time or ourselves. Only the total contribution of all of us can accomplish the task. Together is the only way it can be done. Not an idle hand, for the labourers are so few, and not an idle pound, for the needs are so many.

The money trap

Money can be a booby trap for the unwary. We need pure
hearts, pure motives and God's anointing upon our eyes to
perceive the snares of the Devil. I had hardly started to
reach out to Africa when the Lord sent me a kind of
qualifying test. A lady phoned and invited me to her
house. When I arrived, her home spoke of wealth. It was a
beautiful and opulent place. The owner greeted me with a
warm smile. 'I wanted to meet you so much,' she said,
'because I have watched you for some time.'

She soon came to the point, and it was so wildly beyond
my imagination that I could only stare. She said, 'I want
to finance your gospel crusades in Africa.' I think I forgot
to breathe. On the table was a file which she pushed
across to me. It contained documents setting out her
assets. I read as if I had discovered the Valley of
Eldorado. 'You can see what I have,' she said. 'Iron ore
deposits, a diamond mine, etc....' It was like meeting
Croesus.

'Now,' she explained, 'I want to form a trust and give
half my assets to the work of God. Would you like to join
the trustees? All this money is to be used in the service of
the Lord. Will you accept it?'

Surely God was behind such liberality? Yet I heard no
echo of pleasure from heaven. Instead, I felt a strange
caution, though I tried to hide my lack of enthusiasm. All
I could say was, 'Thank you! But this is a great responsibility. Could I pray about it before committing myself?'

On my arrival home, my wife Anni had the same
reaction. No excitement, but a feeling more like anxiety
instead. We knew we must get down before the Lord
about this and ask for guidance. 'Lord, if this is a trap of
the Devil, I'll have nothing to do with it.'

Occupied with our crusades, weeks passed. We could
say neither yes nor no. Meanwhile, one night I had a
fearful nightmare which I could not forget. I dreamed that
I stood on a river bank at dusk. The water was low,
leaving only puddles and mud. A small man passed me

and walked down the embankment. He beckoned me and I followed. When I was in the middle, suddenly, with an awful roar, a huge hippopotamus rose in front of me. There are two species, and this was the biggest one. I backed away from its engulfing jaws, but there was another of the monsters looming behind me. Others arose from the mud, and I was surrounded on all sides. In peril and despair, I cried out, 'Jesus, help me!' In my dream He did help, and I woke up, but the impression stayed with me.

While that nightmare was still on my mind, the lady contacted me again and pressed me to meet her. She wanted my decision about setting up the trust. We went, and she welcomed us again with a smile. She said, 'Before we go into the house, let me show you around here.' So we walked around her property with her. Her grounds ended at a river, and after a while we came to it. We stood looking across it.

All at once a shock went through me, as if I had been struck by lightning. That river! There it was—the same as in my nightmare. The river was identical, and now I was not dreaming. There was a peril lurking here—that was what the dream meant. God had shown me. I felt the Lord near me, and I was sure my answer was coming. So I asked if we could go into the house and have prayer together.

As soon as we knelt, I heard the voice of the Lord not once, but three times. 'My son, have nothing to do with this.' When we rose, I went to the wealthy lady and said, 'Lady, please, allow me to decline your great generosity. Give your millions to someone else. God does not want me to have this money.' At that moment, a weight seemed to be lifted from my spirit. Why? It seemed so strange. But God did something else at that moment. By His Spirit, He showed me my true assets, the promises in His word. 'My God shall supply all your need according to his riches in glory' (Phil 4:19). I realised that I could exhaust the millions the lady was offering, and when they were finished, my ministry would be finished, also.

Promissory note

This trust fund was not to be my source of supply. God had His own trust. I must do the trusting. In fact, God had planned an even greater source than this lady's fund. I had the divine promissory note—His riches, inexhaustible, backed by His own guarantees. *El Shaddai.* All-sufficient, not penny-pinching. I was more blessed by these precious promises than by all the gold and diamonds in the world.

Somehow, I felt as if I had just passed a very difficult test and had progressed in the school of the Holy Spirit. I had learned that for as long as I would continue to preach the gospel, regardless of how much it cost, the Lord would see that the bills were met. What God orders to be done, He pays for, and if necessary He will move heaven and earth to do it.

Giving royally

I've quoted Philippians 4:19, 'My God shall supply all your needs according to his riches in glory by Christ Jesus.' The phrase 'according to' (from the Greek word *kata*) means 'by the standard of'. That is, by the standard of His riches, not the standard of our poverty. He fills our empty sack, but does not measure it first. He gives as a king does, 'running over'. Not as someone of modest means would be able to give. Don't ask, 'Lord, can You manage to send me £9.50, please? I think I can get by with that. I hope You don't mind.' Tell Him your need. Let Him supply—He has a big hand.

His guests don't sit down to dry crusts; He is the Producer of all the fruit of the field. Giving does not impoverish Him. He always gives. The 'unspeakable gift' of His Beloved Son is God's style of generosity. His scale is worthy of His greatness. He doesn't want His servants to be ill-equipped and threadbare, struggling on like Bob Cratchit for Scrooge.

My visit to that diamond farm hammered something else into my mind. 'Never compromise because of money.' Don't sell your soul for a plate of red porridge.

Later on, when I felt the Lord tell me to order the first big gospel tent, I stood there and said, 'Lord, I am a poor missionary. Look, my pockets are empty.' The Lord replied, 'Don't plan with what is in your pocket, but with what is in Mine.' I looked into His pockets and saw that they were full. I said, 'Lord, if You allow me to plan with what is in Your pockets, then I will plan like a millionaire.' I then began to do so, literally. I've found that God is as rich as He said, and as good. To Him be glory! While doing His perfect will I can ask God, not just for a loaf of bread, but for the whole bakery. His servants don't have to scramble for a piece of the pie, or fight over the crumbs. Look in God's shop window—it is full of cakes.

Twelve baskets full

Tests? Trials of faith? They will come. They come to me, anyway. I remember sitting on the side of my bed in Malawi. I had a three-pounds-a-day room in a Baptist hostel. In fact, I had had to sit down because a shock had just hit me. An urgent phone call from my office in Frankfurt had brought me news I couldn't take in. We were hundreds of thousands of pounds in the red. How could that be?

At the beginning of that year, the Lord had assured me it would be a year of twelve full baskets, a basket for each month. But the baskets had never been so empty. I couldn't see how we could be in debt. 'Lord,' I said, 'why? You said there would be full baskets. But they are all empty. How can that be?'

In such moments, the Lord opens our eyes. He instructed me and said, 'Remember the baskets of the

disciples only started filling *after* the multitudes had all
eaten. Keep on feeding the multitudes with My word and
I will see to filling up the baskets.' I was amazed. The
divine wisdom made sense. I said, 'Lord, I will do what
You say, and I know You will do what You say.'

But hundreds of thousands of pounds.... It seemed
beyond reason. Yes, but God reasons differently. The
baskets stayed empty for twenty-four hours, and then
came the news that God had filled them again. The year
ended without debt. We had just kept on feeding the
multitudes with the word of God, and the Lord had just
kept handing the supplies to us.

When we are breaking the Bread of Life to the spiritually starving, God cannot let us down. That year, we
saw 1,500,000 precious people respond to the call of God
to be saved in our CfaN African crusades alone.

Not a bootlace the world's way

In Genesis, there is a familiar story about Abraham and
Lot. Lot, the nephew of Abraham, had been carried off by
Chedorlaomer after a battle against five kings. One of the
defeated kings was the King of Sodom. Abraham, with
some confederates, went to the rescue and recovered
everything Chedorlaomer had taken, including the captives.

The King of Sodom then started to tell Abraham what
to do with the spoils. 'You keep all the goods and I will
keep the persons.' That was the whole idea in those days.
One country pillaged another, like parasites. But now the
King of Sodom was in for a surprise. Abraham replied: 'I
have lifted up mine hand unto the Lord, the most high
God, the possessor of heaven and earth, that I will not
take from a thread even to a shoelatchet, and that I will
not take any thing that is thine, lest thou shouldest say, I
have made Abram rich' (Gen 14:22–23).

That King had come up against something new in the
world. Abraham was a man with a new way of life—faith

in God. He was one of God's VIPs. In his hands, he held a blueprint for 'a city whose builder and ruler is God'. The way of the world was finished for Abraham. His life had been handed over to God, and he was the Lord's personal responsibility. Abraham had the word and the promise of the Almighty God.

Then God said, 'Abram: I am...thy exceeding great reward' (Gen 15:1). Later, we discover that 'the Lord had blessed Abraham in all things'. All things. That is Bible language, not the world's.

'How shall he not give us all things?' (Romans 8:32).

'All things are yours...' (1 Cor 3:22).

'Your heavenly Father knows you have need of all these things' (Matt 6:32).

'All these things...shall be added unto you' (Matt 6:33).

'His divine power hath given us all things...' (2 Peter 1:3).

That is the Abraham way. Be a child of Abraham! Trust God to the uttermost. He cannot and will not fail.

18

History on the Rope

The eyes of Jesus seem to look at me from behind the lines of print in my Bible, as from a lattice. Everywhere I trace Him I cannot interpret wrongly if His face becomes clearer. I read the following passage. In itself it carries many a lesson, but focus deeper. The story merges with a vaster scene, which I hope you will see as vividly and movingly as the vision appeared to me.

And David was then in an hold, and the garrison of the Philistines was then in Bethlehem. And David longed, and said, 'Oh that one would give me drink of the water of the well of Bethlehem, which is by the gate!' And the three mighty men brake through the host of the Philistines, and drew water out of the well of Bethlehem, that was by the gate, and took it, and brought it to David: nevertheless he would not drink thereof, but poured it out unto the Lord. And he said, 'Be it far from me, O Lord, that I should do this: is not this the blood of the men that went in jeopardy of their lives?' therefore he would not drink it. These things did these three mighty men (2 Sam 23:14–17).

The sigh and the cry for water

David was thirsty and sighed, 'Oh that one would give me drink of the water of the well of Bethlehem, which is by the gate!' That particular well, however, was situated behind enemy lines. The Philistines held it. Standing near, within earshot as David spoke his inner wish out loud, were several of his best warriors. To them, David's wish was their command. Three of them looked at one another, nodded to each other and formed an instant partnership. Without a further word, they set out together on a special mission to fulfil David's desire.

They knew the dangers. They may have to pay for a cup of water for David with their life blood. But such considerations gave them not a moment's hesitation. Protest and complaint were out of the question. What David wanted must be supplied, even though he would never have sent them himself. David was their lord. They knew his mind and that was enough. Risks were their common duty. Loyalty does not wait for orders. Hesitation would suggest that they were reluctant to please their leader.

The wish of David for a drink brings to mind the far more important words of Jesus as He hung on the cross. He also cried, 'I thirst.' His thirst was, no doubt, physical, but it reached beyond the physical. His great thirst was for the salvation of men and women. It was that thirst which brought Him to earth and to the cross. His physical thirst was only the result of His infinite desire for the souls of His creatures.

That cry from the cross of, 'I thirst,' rings in our ears for ever, having a far deeper meaning than David's, 'I thirst.' How many recognise that fact? Have we ears to hear, or do we conveniently not catch the true import of those two words? Do we give serious attention to that cry from the cross, allowing it to move our hearts and our lives to action? Is that cry being heard now by anyone?

For a wish little more than a whim, David's men set out to please him. They could have brought water from a safer place, perhaps better water, in fact, but that would not have satisfied their sense of utter devotion to their lord. For David, they did not count their lives dear to them.

I am challenged. How many of us would be as ready to act similarly for our Lord Jesus? We know His desire— the salvation of souls—but do we need urgings and commands before we acknowledge it? Isn't a knowledge of His thirst our obligation to act? The desires of the Son of God—what could be a louder call? Even if it should mean putting our lives at risk, remember that men risked their lives for a mere cup of water for David. And how often is danger involved, anyhow, in fulfilling the desire of the Son of God?

The well of Bethlehem

The well of Bethlehem was surrounded by enemy troops. But David's three warriors took their swords, along with their water vessel, and began their exploit. The well was sunk very deep into the ground, which increased the danger involved. The precious waters were deep down, yet this was the water David longed for. Somebody had to go down and bring it up.

What a vivid picture of our present situation. Multitudes who are in the depths of darkness have to be reached. They must be brought up to the light, going from death to life. Whole nations are in spiritual graves. Somebody has to go down and do the job. The well of Bethlehem was in Philistine hands. This meant that the warriors first had to break through enemy lines. There was a skirmish and then a breakthrough. Those three men were driven and strengthened by their determination to bring their commander-in-chief something they merely had overheard was his wish.

Holding the rope

A water well normally has some mechanical means with which to heave up the water. But, in order to connect with

our New Testament picture, let us imagine that there were
no such means. Those three men were faced with a very
hard task when they arrived at the well. The warriors had
to organise themselves and decide who should go down
the well. It meant that while one went down on a rope, the
others would have to hold him.

This is certainly the only way when it comes to world
evangelism. Teamwork is absolutely essential. World outreach today needs, and always has needed, those who are
willing to go down and those who are willing to hold the
rope. That rope is the support line of the ones who have
gone down, and those who hold it are just as important as
those who go down. The supporters dare not slacken their
hold on the rope until the man with the water is all the
way up. That rope is a lifeline. Not even a tea break is
possible for those who are holding it. Any relaxation of
grip, and the man depending on that rope is lost. Those
precious men and women who go out at the desire of
Jesus, in order to bring Him the waters He longs for, are in
exactly the same position. Without the rope holders (the
supporters), tragedy would take place.

Logistics

It is a most serious matter when anyone today says that
we should cut back on our commitment to world evangelism. Due to pressing domestic economic problems, world
need is pushed aside for local need. My deep conviction is
this: we cannot afford to slacken our hands on the rope of
support for those who have risked so much for the task.
Too much depends on their efforts. The missionaries
themselves depend on that lifeline, and, even more
importantly, the whole gospel project of Christ (which is
His water), also must reach our heavenly David.

These are kingdom of God logistics. It is as simple as
one, two, three. I myself praise God for the men and
women who back us with prayer and intercession, thus
keeping the tension on the rope. I certainly remember

many days when I have been in the darkness of those wells or pits across the world, and have felt the presence of the hosts of hell. Yet, every time, I knew that there were faithful prayer partners who held the rope and stood with me night and day. Thank God for these rope holders!

Eventually, the warrior on the end of the rope was pulled out of the well. In his hands he held the container with the precious water. All three men rejoiced and immediately began their journey back. I can imagine that the two flanked the one carrying the precious water on his left and right sides. How carefully the warrior carried the vessel. Under no circumstances did he want to lose one drop of what he had gone to fetch. The men on each side had their swords in their hands, and they opened the way for the middle man. It was perfect teamwork.

The kingdom of God also depends so much upon the union of Holy Ghost anointed ministries. Evangelism and missions require the sum total of all contributory effort. 'Like a mighty army moves the church of God,' we sing, but this needs to be a reality if we are to fulfil the Great Commission.

Heroes

The warriors finally arrived at the tent of David, their lord, with the water and their blood-stained swords. Then—he refused to drink the water! He realised that they had risked their very blood to bring it to him. However, it is a fact that David ranked all three of these men as heroes. Some might have honoured only the one who had gone down into the pit, but not so with David. All three warriors had a vital part in bringing about this victory.

One day, we will kneel before our heavenly David. All God's children will be there—those who went down into the pits, as well as those who held the ropes faithfully. I am sure that we will witness many great surprises. Those who had been so inconspicuous will all of a sudden be heroes in the kingdom of God. Their reward will be great.

The Lord will say, 'Well done, thou good and faithful servant.'

A cleaner a hero?

A pastor in Germany told me of one lady in his church whose job it was to clean the church building after use. She came to him and said that she had had a wonderful dream. She dreamed she stood before the gate of eternity. Many people were lined up, and she joined them. Then she realised that all the people in front of her held sheaves in their arms, while she presented only a few ears of wheat. She felt very uncomfortable and let others, who came behind her, get in front. Then, suddenly, the gate opened and her name was called. It was the Lord. Trembling, she stepped forward with those pitiful ears in her hand. But the Lord spoke comforting words to her: 'You have been faithful over few, I will put you over much.' Then she woke up. The pastor told me that exactly a week after this dream, the lady died. I was deeply touched. Holding the rope is not always glamorous, but it surely is worth the while. 'It will be worth it all, when we see Jesus.'

Let us not relax. Keep on bringing to Jesus the 'water' that will quench His thirst. He thirsts—He desires to have with Him, in His salvation kingdom, men and women, boys and girls. He longs for them to hear and accept the gospel. That is what evangelism is all about.

Although the pit is deeper and darker than ever, we will be more productive than ever, *if* we work hand in hand. God is faithful. If we are to fulfil the word of the Lord, we must be ready to go down to the lost, or else be ready to keep our hands firmly grasping the supporting rope.

History on the end of a rope

The men from David's army were not the only men who held on to ropes. We remember that Jeremiah, the great prophet, was pulled from the pit, and that Joseph's rescue from a pit eventually prevented famine in that ancient world. There were men who, when his life was at stake, let Paul down over the wall of Damascus. All these helpers only grasped ropes, yet they all held future history in their hands.

Suppose Joseph had been left in the pit? What would have happened to Egypt and to Jacob's family, as well as to a future son of Jacob, our Lord Jesus? It is quite awful to think this thought through to the end.

Suppose Jeremiah had not been rescued, and that his work had perished with him in that horrible pit? Would we have had his prophecies, and would Israel have, through these long centuries, drawn the comfort and hope which was theirs through his words? A world without any memory of Jeremiah, without his wonderful books in the Bible—imagine it! But somebody held the rope and Jeremiah was rescued.

Suppose the apostle Paul had not escaped those seeking to assassinate him, or that his rope holders had let his basket crash and kill him. He was the man who brought Christianity to Europe. If they had known that the destinies of nations dangled on the end of that one little rope, how much tighter might they have gripped it! But they held on strongly enough, and we are eternally blessed, thanks to them.

I am convinced in my heart that those who are rope holders in world evangelism today are making history for time and eternity. Can you feel the pull? Do you hear the multitudes calling upon the name of the Lord for salvation? Do you see that massive exodus from the kingdom of darkness into the marvellous light of God? These precious souls saved are the future citizens of the New Jerusalem. Today we cannot afford to reduce global efforts to bring the gospel of salvation to the nations. We dare not do less, but must do more. Too much is at stake. The eternity of millions depends on what we do today.

At the same time, I would like to thank all those faithful men and women who have been, and are, our rope holders. This is true for those who have given prayer and/ or financial support. Some glorious morning, when we kneel at the feet of Jesus, they will receive their real reward.

Our support is for whom? We cannot tell, but somebody, somewhere, is holding a new future in their hands for many—possibly for the whole world. To save a world, hold the rope—that is all that you may be asked to do, but it is critically vital. To lose a world, don't bother to lend a hand—that is all you have to do.

19

Integrity: The Satanic Target

The beginning is in the end

When I was a young minister, I attended a pastors' conference where there was great blessing. The power of God fell and we went down on our knees before the Lord. An old servant of God in his nineties knelt next to me, and he prayed with such earnestness that I couldn't help but hear and watch him. This is what he prayed: 'Lord, forgive me where I have allowed those things in my life and ministry that were not clean....'

This prayer moved me deeply. I was touched. I had to follow his prayer with a prayer of my own. 'Lord, help me, please. May I never allow anything unclean in my life and ministry. Help me so that when I am old I need not pray a prayer like my precious brother has prayed.'

I would say this today, my dear fellow ministers. Hear the word of the Lord. 'We must mind in the beginning what matters in the end. Carry your very souls in your hands and walk circumspectly.'

Satanic strategy

Christians who are at the forefront are prime targets for Satan—and for attacks of the media, as well. Neither the Devil nor the press are shining examples of accuracy or mercy. Satanic hatred has scored off of some of God's servants lately. The tragedies of sin have been welcome copy to the scandal sheets, which covered the indiscretions with full orchestration. David wrote a poetic lament mourning the death of his mortal foe, King Saul. But modern writers are smaller men, of less nobility and civilisation. They often maximise the damage to the kingdom of God.

I want to put you on your guard. The Devil is very patient. He is implacable. Hell will brood and plot for years, engineering circumstances. Demon powers will try every devious means to encompass and destroy a believer's testimony. The Devil is a full-time professional opponent. Christ repulsed him, so, biding his time, the Devil attacked the disciples (Lk 22:31). Judas betrayed Jesus, Peter denied Him with oaths and curses, and the rest forsook the Lord and fled, right at His crisis hour (Mt 26:56). Incredible!

The Enemy may lull us into a sense of false immunity. Mild temptations resisted help deceive us about our moral strength. Then Satan turns his big guns upon our unguarded flanks—just where we thought we were so strong. Guard your 'strong' points. We can despise those who fall, which is a way of drawing attention to our own superior holiness. Remember—better men have fallen. Never underestimate satanic subtlety. Only saving grace preserves our feet from slipping.

If you consider spiritual warfare, remember that its main battleground is in your own heart and mind, not up in the skies somewhere. 'Keep thy heart with all diligence; for out of it are the issues of life' (Prov 4:23). Before you go into combat daily, 'Watch and pray that ye enter not into temptation.'

Right at the start, make a covenant with God to live a

holy life. But remember that determination alone will not do it. Success in and of yourself is not guaranteed, even with a contract written with a pen dipped in your very blood. 'The arm of flesh will fail you.' I want to point out a better way.

A celestial example of perfect service

'He is able to keep us from falling' (Jude 24). But how? That is the frequent question. How can we serve perfectly? A key is found in Isaiah 6:

> In the year that king Uzziah died I saw also the Lord sitting upon a throne, high and lifted up, and his train filled the temple. Above it stood the seraphims: each one had six wings; with twain he covered his face, and with twain he covered his feet, and with twain he did fly. And one cried unto another, and said, 'Holy, holy, holy, is the Lord of hosts: the whole earth is full of his glory' (vv 1–3).

Now the seraphims are throne angels of the Most High. Nothing sullied would be allowed so close to God and the seat of all power in heaven, on earth, and under the earth. Isaiah saw these celestial intelligences serving the Lord in the holiest place of all, the atmosphere of God's immediate presence. Somewhere here is a challenge to purity, along with the way to achieve it. These creatures are our models.

The noticeable feature about these seraphims is that they each had six wings. Two wings covered their faces, which speaks of humility. Two wings covered their feet, which speaks of purity. With two wings they flew, which speaks of worship and praise.

Humility

First, why did these mighty beings cover their glorious and beautiful faces and prevent the young prophet Isaiah from seeing them? It was so they would not prevent him from seeing the Lord. Here is an important significance in this account. The seraphims would not 'upstage' the Lord and distract Isaiah's gaze from the throne.

Notice, also, that though they were the most holy of creatures themselves, they only spoke of the holiness of the Lord and of His glory. Humility is part of holiness.

The same lesson comes from the Mount of Transfiguration (Mt 17:1–8). In those marvellous moments, Moses and Elijah appeared. We read, however, that presently the disciples saw Jesus only, the two prophets having withdrawn from view. The Father's interest, too, was similar. He did not talk to the disciples about the two great prophets of Israel. The Father said, 'This is my beloved Son, in whom I am well pleased; hear ye him' (v 5).

Jesus Christ, the Son of God, is the centre, the focus for all. Every miracle comes from Him. What room is there for human pride? These heavenly seraphs, princes of glory burning like flames, hid their own attractions. Moses and Elijah, appearing in their glory, giants among redeemed immortals, retired into the background. What then we fragile and fading earth folk? Aim to dazzle and you dim God's glory. Preach for personal admiration and people who come to see God will only see the preacher.

Here lies a spiritual risk for all servants of the Lord. Are we working for recognition or to make a name for ourselves? Do we just want 'big meetings' to use the tens of thousands of people for a backdrop to highlight our own imagined greatness? The light from the cross is not the limelight for any preacher. Jesus Christ did not die to give us a career, but to save the lost. What did the great evangelist and apostle Paul say? 'For though I preach the gospel, I have nothing to glory of: for necessity is laid upon me: yea, woe is unto me, if I preach not the gospel!' (1 Cor 9:16).

The character of John the Baptist should lead us to a sobering view of ourselves. Such was his stature that some wondered if he was the Messiah himself. Even Christ said John was the greatest born of women. When more people began to turn to Christ than were following John's ministry, John's followers were jealous. But John wasn't. He told them that Jesus must increase, and he declared, 'I must decrease.' When half the nation came, he pointed away from himself to Jesus. At the river he cried, 'Behold the Lamb of God!' Every single thing that John said about himself was a declaration of his own lowliness. Greatness begins and ends with humility. That is what it means to cover one's face.

The Lord is a jealous God. 'My glory I will not give to another.' To be proud in the presence of the King of kings is to touch the very Ark of God, a sin for which Uzzah died (2 Sam 6:6). Herod, puffed up like a bull frog with a toad, a crowd shouting that he was a god, was struck down. 'Because he gave not the glory to God', he was 'eaten of worms', a terrible disease known by doctors today (Acts 12:21–23).

Those privileged to exercise the gifts of the Spirit must be especially careful. Show-offs will be shown up. Spiritual gifts are not oscars for display won as trophies of performance. Don't decorate yourself ostentatiously with God's power tools. Don't make tiaras, necklaces and rings from the spiritual gifts for your own adornment.

The sentry of your heart's door is called 'Humility'. Dismiss that guardian and the unprotected gate is soon battered in, with the Enemy taking over.

Purity is next to probity

The second pair of wings covered the seraphims' feet. This action signified purity. The cleanest man makes contact with the ground as he walks. There was no dust near the throne, of course, but the seraphs' act was symbolic. It signalled the need to walk in holiness before the Lord.

Jesus made a special point of this. He stooped to wash the feet of the disciples. Such cleansing was needed. He said, 'He that is washed needeth not but to wash his feet, but is clean every whit.'

First, we must watch where we walk—make no preparation for the works of the flesh, Paul suggests. Don't pray, 'Lead us not into temptation,' and then land yourself in it. Unclean feet are the symbol of a careless walk. 'Be ye clean that bear the vessels of the Lord.'

That is wise, as of course we all know. Such advice, though, is given more glibly than taken. The modern media pour moral pollution into the atmosphere, like chimneys belching soot. We need a gas mask not to breathe in the soul diseases of a materialistic age with its accompanying unbelief. Diligence is one thing, certainly, but we need other help. What is it?

Our best safeguard is using the word to wash our minds constantly. Our thought life, conditioned by the word of God and the covering of the blood of Jesus, is impregnable. 'Gird up the loins of your mind' (1 Pet 1:13) by the daily reading of the word. It is an immunisation injection against all spiritual infections. 'Thy word have I hid in mine heart, that I might not sin against thee' (Ps 119:11). Scientists have produced a polish for cars which simply rejects dirt. Long before such scientific experiments, believers found that the power of the word repulses sin.

How can we do what Scripture says—'Whatsoever things are lovely, think on these things'? To begin with, the Bible gives us things that are lovely to think on as well as fortifying to our desires and motives. Pray also, 'Lead us not into temptation,' and 'watch and pray'. And never presume you do not need to do so.

Then you can stand before men with an open countenance on any platform; your motives transparent, with no shame to conceal—an experience that is worth everything. Better still, you can have confidence as you stand before God. We often hear of Esau selling his birthright for a bowl of pottage, but a whole generation of Israel lost the Promised Land and died in the wilderness bemoaning the cucumbers of Egypt. Don't lose everything for a passing pleasure. God warned Israel that they would receive 'the fruit of their thoughts', a terrible warning, and so it was bound to happen and eventually did (Jer 6:19). A man's true character is his mind.

Worship and praise

'They flew', we read, with their third pair of wings. As they flew, they cried out, saying, 'Holy, holy, holy, is the Lord of hosts: the whole earth is full of his glory.' They flew and sang—that was worship. The beat of their wings was music. Just a brief remark: it is amazing that these heavenly beings didn't cry, 'Love, love, love…' or, 'Peace, peace, peace…', but, 'Holy, holy, holy, is the Lord of hosts….' The highest zenith of praise and the highest form of worship are always connected with the holiness and glory of God.

How could these angels say that the whole earth is full of God's glory? Had they never heard of heathen and atheistic empires, of war, hatred, greed and suffering? Yes, of course they had, but they saw them from a higher viewpoint as they flew before the throne. They had God's perspective, not the human view. Soaring above the earthly scene, the total situation revealed, they burst into rapturous exclamation. Scanning horizons beyond the sight of earth dwellers, the skies of all tomorrows, they sang, 'The whole earth is full of his glory.'

Get the throne perspective. What is your angle? Have you a molehill aspect or the Everest view? Are you a flatlander with a two-dimensional outlook? Or are you a dweller on the spiritual highlands who has God's dimension added?

You ascend to God's throne when you praise and worship. Praise lifts you. Doubt and murmuring, instead of wings of song, are boots of lead on your feet. In worship we contemplate the throne, the power of the Lord, and his holiness. There we rest under His protection.

In the throne room Isaiah was equipped, sent and cleansed with the altar fire in order to be God's servant with perfect integrity. Glory to God! When we serve the Lord with pure motive, rejoicing in His presence before His throne, we are invincible, impregnable. Trouble starts when we lose the throne perspective. But, elevated by worship to the third dimension, our character will be armour-plated.

The second key—an earthly example

I am setting out the following scripture to be sure you will read it. Ponder it carefully and reverently. Let the Holy Spirit burn it into your soul.

> Behold, here I am: witness against me before the Lord, and before his anointed: whose ox have I taken? or whose ass have I taken? or whom have I defrauded? whom have I oppressed? or of whose hand have I received any bribe to blind mine eyes therewith? and I will restore it you (1 Sam 12:3).

This bold challenge was part of the farewell speech of Samuel before Israel. The Judges period of Israel ended with Samuel, who was by far the finest of these charismatic deliverers. His words, which I have quoted here, are, for their times, amazing. In those early days, petty oppressions were regarded as simply a ruler's perks, and sheer tyranny surprised no one. For Samuel to be able to make a public challenge of his own probity gives him a stature unequalled among the world's leaders.

Samuel's duty to govern and to deal with wrongdoers was absolute, and his judgements were without appeal. Those upon whom he had imposed penalties could have held a grudge against him and been very vindictive. His public words would have given them their opportunity. They could have spoken and claimed that he had done them ill.

A prototype to follow

So what happened? Samuel's reputation was so high that he had no fear. The massed representatives of the nation roared out, 'Thou hast not defrauded us, nor oppressed us, neither hast thou taken aught of any man's hand.' He had judged all and now all judged him innocent, an unflawed man of God. A genuine prototype to follow.

Samuel had never taken a bribe or advantage on one single occasion for a period of half a century or more. Such behaviour did not come only from being scrupulously thoughtful. In the heat of the moment, such restraint is not always possible. His heart was right, and that was his secret. Honesty had become his natural instinct as a man filled with God and with God's word. Perhaps without time to consider, acting automatically, he nonetheless never put a foot wrong.

However, the unanimous testimony of Israel was not enough for Samuel. He knew that people, in fact sometimes all the people, can be fooled, impressed by a mere pose. For Samuel, only one judgement really mattered: that of the Lord. We read, 'Samuel called unto the Lord; and the Lord sent thunder and rain that day: and all the people greatly feared the Lord and Samuel' (1 Sam 12:18).

It meant God thundered His endorsement of His servant. It was harvest time, the dry season. But when the Lord's anointed prophet raised his arms and asked for heaven's vote, a miracle happened. The sky quickly filled with clouds and then came lightning, thunder and rain. This was God's 'Amen' approving Samuel's integrity.

The people crouched in awe before such a supernatural display. God had exposed the heart of Samuel to them all. Throughout the humdrum, everyday duties and affairs of the people, Samuel always had acted with rectitude. In his handling of money and every small judgement and decision, when nobody would have seen, there had never been a bad or rotten deal.

Now God brought it to light and sealed it. Moreover, God gave a revelation of what it meant. He was with Samuel, and He and this man were as one. Samuel had a greatness with the greatness of the Lord, so that the very heavens responded to testify. Shady dealings, along with petty and sordid tricks, had no place in Samuel's record. Samuel's honesty linked him with the authority of God.

That which is impure and shabby puts us outside the realm of the Spirit. God Himself will approve us when we keep both feet within the kingdom of God. Power, glory and blessing will show earthly desire to be a murky shadow. The Almighty Himself embraces the cause of a man who can stand up and declare his integrity before the whole world, unafraid to ask the Samuel questions. The time to begin these godly practices is right now, at the beginning of one's ministry, not after having learned these truths by bitter experience. Even if you have sinned in this area, you can begin living in integrity right now.

The third key—anointed footsteps

Here is my third scripture key:

> It is like the precious ointment upon the head, that ran down upon the beard, even Aaron's beard: that went down to the skirts of his garments (Ps 133:2).

What an anointing—so copious. That sacred oil flowed down his robes and dripped onto his feet and onto the floor. The ointment was specially prepared for the High Priest alone, and it carried its own unique perfume. Wherever Aaron walked, the oil on his feet and that which still dripped from the skirts of his garments marked his movements. People could recognise his footsteps as those of the High Priest.

May God grant that even after we have left this world we shall leave behind anointed footsteps for generations to come. The anointing of God upon you gives you the walk of Aaron. These memories of integrity in a man of God are better than an inscription on the finest marble. Anointed men and women make history which is everlasting in the kingdom of God.

20

Battering Rams of Intercession

Behind the scenes

What a privileged evangelist is the one who has intercessors behind him. They are the munition workers providing the dynamite for our gospel bombardment of hell. Intercessors are more than prayer partners, as we shall see. They are a Moses kind of people.

In some ways we can never be like Moses. He was a prince, law-giver, nation-maker and genius. But he was something even greater which we *can* be. He was an intercessor. As an Egyptian prince, Moses was trained in warfare and probably even commanded soldiers. But when Israel's existence was threatened, Moses himself turned to intercession. He defended his people by pleading their cause with God. He put no confidence in the arm of the flesh, but went on his face before the Lord.

Forty years earlier, Moses had taken things upon himself while trying to deliver Israel. He struck the first blow for their freedom, but the blow was a failure. Moses had to flee. At the end of his career, he again asserted himself in a way which the Bible describes as unbelief. The discontent

214

of the people pushed him to extremes. He stood and arrogantly demanded, 'Must we fetch you water out of this rock?' (Num 20:10). Then God removed him. He had exceeded his authority and forsaken his secret.

The world has its techniques to sway the masses. Great crowds gather in our services. But I trust that the unworthy methods of crowd psychology and the tricks of the rabble-rouser are a thousand miles beneath us. We have another method, Moses' secret—intercession. Who equalled the effectiveness of Moses in that ancient world—or does today? Episode after episode illustrates Moses' power. Moses saw God, and as a man lived with that vision. Today, some may consider him a primitive. Three thousand years have passed, but who has surpassed his influence on mankind? His impact on history is greater than anyone's, except for Christ's. Such rich results move me to go back and watch this prince with God. Just take one instance, from Exodus 17:8–16.

> Then came Amalek, and fought with Israel in Rephidim. And Moses said unto Joshua, 'Choose us out men, and go out, fight with Amalek: tomorrow I will stand on the top of the hill with the rod of God in mine hand.' So Joshua did as Moses had said to him, and fought with Amalek: and Moses, Aaron and Hur went up to the top of the hill. And it came to pass, when Moses held up his hand, that Israel prevailed: and when he let down his hand, Amalek prevailed. But Moses' hands were heavy; and they took a stone, and put it under him, and he sat thereon; and Aaron and Hur stayed up his hands, the one on the one side, and the other on the other side; and his hands were steady until the going down of the sun. And Joshua discomfited Amalek and his people with the edge of the sword. And the Lord said unto Moses, 'Write this for a memorial in a book, and rehearse it in the ears of Joshua: for I will utterly put out the remembrance of Amalek from under heaven.'

Some don't pray. They call it a mystery and write prayer off. Yet they certainly make use of other things which they don't understand. Why Amalek prevailed when Moses' arms became heavy may seem strange. Prayer is not a matter of logic, though, but of revelation. All throughout history, men have found that God answers prayer. There is no use in arguing with the way things are. Just enjoy them! This instance (of Moses holding up his hands before God) was ordered by the Lord to be 'written in a book', and from this Book, the Bible, we can take our instructions.

Reaching the heart of God

First, intercession was wrought in Moses' heart. In fact, there were no words of Moses recorded in this incident. His prayer was not a formal, correct litany, or a say-it-word-for-word formula. Moses spoke not a word, but his spirit strove with God, and he expressed it by lifting his hands. Aaron and Hur shared in this victory by supporting his arms. The heart of God is reached by our hearts, not by mere sounds from our lips. But we nonetheless must express ourselves, and Moses really put himself into his supplications physically. The apostle Paul wrote, 'I will therefore that men pray every where, lifting up holy hands' (1 Tim 2:8). The intensity of Moses perhaps was too great for mere words, but we cannot usually plead in silence. In the same chapter, Paul writes, 'I exhort therefore, that...supplications, prayers, intercessions and giving of thanks be made for all men' (1 Tim 2:1).

Battering rams of intercession

Secondly, one man lifted his hands, but two men helped him to do so. There has been so much said about 'a man to stand in the gap', but the years pass and who can point to such a man? If anybody claimed he was that man, he would certainly be considered unique. Others must be in on the act. In fact, this story shows they must be. We cannot leave the praying to one man or to one woman, or to a few so-called prayer warriors. Do not say, 'It's only a prayer meeting.' Let the millions gather to storm the citadel of sin.

In our CfaN gospel crusades we follow this principle. Suzette Hattingh is a vital, key member of the CfaN team. Much insight in this chapter must be credited to her. Her special ministry is not merely to sign up prayer partners, but actually to gather together thousands, instructing and leading them in true intercession. It is not a case of singing choruses and praying for a blessing, but of pulling down the strongholds of Satan. Intercessors are mighty battering rams.

We are not bothered about fine words, but with the expression of the heart. People may kneel, sit, stand, lie down before the Lord or walk around, though all under overall leadership. There is no waiting while the pastor pleads, 'Someone please lead us in prayer.' Instead, everyone prays together, just as in the Acts of the Apostles. There is liberty, but not licence; freedom, but not extravagance. Every gathering must have order and respect it. But we are not afraid of people calling upon God and crying out to him, even with tears.

Touch-point on earth of heavenly power

Thirdly, Amalek felt a satanic hostility against Israel, and that enmity was met by the spiritual forces of prayer. Amalek would seem to have had no reason for the attack. The assault was Devil-inspired and quite irrational. Only a spiritual power could resist it.

We have exactly the same situation today. The enemies of the gospel walk 'according to the prince of the power of the air, the spirit that now worketh in the children of disobedience' (Eph 2:2). This is the spirit of the age. We must come to grips spiritually with this in order for that power to be broken. Good sermons or discussion alone will never do the job. Evil lies deep. Drive it out of its burrows by the all-prevailing weapon of prayer and supplication. Enter into Calvary victory. ' "By my Spirit," saith the

Lord.' Intercession is like a lightning conductor, the touch-point on earth of heavenly power.

Relationship between prayer and events

Fourthly, the battle was won by Moses, Aaron and Hur on the mountain top, together with Joshua and his men below. The tide of battle did not ebb and flow according to Joshua's strategy, but according to the intercession of these men. From the account, it seems that Moses occasionally lowered his arms, with Amalek prevailing until he lifted them again. Those who fought on the hilltop and those who struggled in the valley were one. The relationship between prayer and events was clearly demonstrated.

In the palm of his hand

Fifthly, Moses lifted up his hands. I pointed out that Moses did not intercede alone. But there is something more, something which concerns Moses' five fingers. Suzette Hattingh says that one day, she suddenly realised that the five offices named in Ephesians 4 were like fingers on a hand. Each finger functions on its own, but only when connected to the palm of a hand. That palm represents the body of Christ. Intercession is a function of the body, an assignment for all believers, not just a task of the fingers of the hand or the special gift of men whom Jesus gives to the church. All members of the body of Christ should intercede—this is the principle we employ in our crusades.

How it is done

For six to eight weeks before a crusade, Suzette involves as many members of the body of Christ as possible in intense intercession. No single champion prays alone, but instead the whole church puts its weight behind the onslaught. The gates of hell are stormed, and we knock on the doors of heaven in supplication. We do this expressly for the salvation of souls and the moving of God's Spirit.

The intensity of such intercession does not climax and conclude when the crusade starts. It is continued right up to the altar call. Hundreds, sometimes even thousands, pray and are engaged in spiritual warfare during our crusade meetings. At the very time the evangelist is working, preaching and ministering, those behind the scenes are dealing with spiritual forces to help obtain the evangelist's victory. It is just like Moses praying for Joshua while the latter was in the thick of the battle. If intercession is not needed at that time, when the satanic onslaught is greatest, then when is it needed?

In the Bible account in Exodus 17, the two groups, Israel's army and Moses' companions, were in separate places, yet together fought the same battle at the same time. In our evangelistic meetings, the intercessors also may be away from the crusade grounds, praying in a field away from the main site or in a different hall. But these prayer warriors are an active part of the evangelistic meeting itself, upholding the evangelist and joining with the armies of heaven to push back the powers of darkness.

The effectiveness of this strategy certainly has been proved. With this intercessory backing the Enemy must withdraw, leaving unconverted people open to the power of the word of God. There is a great harvest of souls, an edification of the body of Christ and a fulfilment of the word of God. We all thus become partners with Christ and shareholders in His harvest. Our intercessors hold back the armies of Satan until souls are safe inside the kingdom of God.

This strategy originated with God, and is therefore blessed by Him. It affects the individual Christian, the churches, the city, the country and above all the unbeliever. Intercession builds a highway for the evangelism that wins the world.

The meaning

Just as Moses and Joshua worked together in the battle, so
the Lord always has intended for intercession and evangelism to function in combination. Intercession and evangelism are one in battle. They are like a hand in a glove, or
water on a river bed, or branches in a vine.

Intercession that is not linked to soul-saving is like an
arrow shot without a target, an athlete running a race
which has no finish line, or a football match without a goal
net. If we pray for revival, we should do something about
it. Also, intercession is preparatory work; a plough breaking up the ground for the sowing and the harvest. That
does not mean we should not intercede until a crusade or
similar work is arranged, but it certainly means that we
should have a vision and a plan of outreach.

Then there is the other omission—evangelism without
intercessory prayer. It is like cranking machinery by hand
with no power supply, or fishing without a net and trying
to catch the fish one by one, by the tail.

Your rightful inheritance

The attack by Amalek was an attempt by the heathen to
keep Israel out of their inheritance. That highlights the
proper theme of intercessory effort, set out for us in Psalm
2:8: 'Ask of me, and I shall give thee the heathen for thine
inheritance, and the uttermost parts of the earth for thy
possession.'

Note: we first *ask* (intercede), and then afterwards *possess*. Intercession is followed by evangelism—actually
going into the land and possessing it. The same principle
is shown in 1 Timothy 2:1, where we are told to make
intercession for all men. But it has a definite target, as
verse 4 states. The aim is for 'all men to be saved, and to
come unto the knowledge of the truth'. Take note of the
phrase 'all men'. That is how a world can be saved—
through intercession and evangelism.

We also ought to notice that Moses sat down. He did

not excuse himself with, 'I'm tired,' for 'men ought always to pray, and not to faint' (Lk 18:1) and 'not be weary in well doing' (Gal 6:9). He settled himself to pray until victory came, not governed by the clock. It is a matter of taking up a specific battle area, not of praying in a general sort of way or of fasting for no particular reason. Spending time in prayer is a proper duty, but intercession involves a blow directed against a recognised foe.

Furthermore, and very importantly, Moses did not just say a prayer. His hands stayed up until Joshua had routed Amalek. It was intercession and persistence that secured the victory. Suzette calls it 'travail'. She gives such definitions as these to intercession:

To pray that God's will be done in the world.

To intervene, mediate and work with God.

To be part of what God is doing, to serve Him in prayer.

To pray God's burden and not our own opinions. What He wants, not what we think we should pray, thereby 'taking on the mind of Christ'.

To see the need for God's action and then, with boldness and confidence, to ask that He act.

Definitions

Suzette points out that the word 'intercession' actually first appears in Isaiah 53:12, when it speaks of Christ who 'made intercession for the transgressors'. The Hebrew is *baga,* from the root meaning 'to impinge with violence'. 'Impinge' means 'to collide with'. Vine's Dictionary states that *baga* means 'to strike up against, to be violent against, to invade, to come between, to cause to entreat, to meet with, and pray'.

So there are two separate aspects here: warfare and travail. First, *baga* means really facing Satan in the name of Jesus on behalf of people, thereby 'striking up against' and colliding with him. The word also implies travail, which is gentle—'to come between', or to face the Father on behalf of people. Intercession thus has two features: facing Satan and facing God.

Suzette also draws attention to the words for intercession used in the New Testament. One Greek word has two parts, the first meaning 'exceeding', and the other part meaning 'to meet on behalf of or for someone's sake'. In other words, reaching across and doing our utmost for others. Another word for intercession implies 'to get the ear of the King on behalf of others'. That shows that close fellowship is needed.

Suzette also directs us to an ordinary dictionary (in this case, Webster's). Intercession is described as 'mediation, entreaty, prayer or petition on behalf of another', and the verb 'intercede' is defined as 'an act between parties with a view to reconciling their differences or points of contention, to mediate, to plead or to interpose on behalf of another'. Entreaty, petition, plead, intervene, interpose— that is prayer raised to its highest temperature.

Phineas intervened when Israel grossly sinned and a plague broke out throughout the land. The spreading terror was checked, and it was counted to Phineas as righteousness for generations afterwards. Intercession involves being a peacemaker, bringing men and women into the peace of God. It raises a harvest of righteousness which counts for eternity. That is the power which lies in intercession.

It is important, Suzette emphasises, to have the direction of God for our praying. We must have His target. God needs channels for what He wants. Suzette strongly insists that we must know His concerns, for He knows what is happening when we do not, and is well aware of where Satan is mustering his attack.

The intercessor's secrets

The Lord also may give us burdens for tasks we should do ourselves, like speaking to a person about some personal matter. The main purpose of intercession, however, is not to hear secrets about others from God. We should not go around 'straightening out' the body, telling people what God thinks and sharing His confidences with everyone. (Suzette calls this 'spiritual gossip' and warns that God's secrets are holy unto the Lord.) God tells us certain information so that we can intercede for others, thereby bringing about the purposes He has for them. The Lord seems to share such secrets only about 2% of the time, however. The other 98% of intercession time is spent turning the world back to God as we are led by the Spirit.

Taking up the work of an intercessor is a life-changing experience, but only God can build an intercessor. If the Lord brings you through experiences which turn your desire to clamour at the throne of God for our lost world, you will not regret it, however hard the preparation work may have been.

Intercession changes your life's attitudes, bringing you a fulfilment which nobody can describe to you beforehand, as it is so rich. Put your heart at God's disposal, not just your time alone, and you will have put your treasure where no moth can take hold.

Evangelism must be seen as the work of the Holy Spirit in every single sense. All aspects of an evangelistic campaign are yielded to Him—the preaching, the singing, the order of the meeting, the use of every ministry and the gifts of the Spirit. It is one great effort, backed by local believers as well as the church at large. Evangelism removes every blockage, every hindering self-motive and every device which may keep men from God. Evangelism is the Holy Spirit working through both intercession and ministry. Such a combination brings about the revival which is conquering the world.

Christ For All Nations

In 1967, Reinhard and Anni Bonnke left Germany for the continent of Africa. They brought little with them besides their baby son, Freddy, and hearts burning with the desire to reach people with the gospel. Even then, the drive was strong. Reinhard would attract crowds at the main bus terminal by playing his accordian and singing gospel songs, then he would preach his heart out to them.

Then, in 1972, Reinhard was gripped by a recurring vision. Night after night, he saw the vast continent of Africa being washed in the blood of Jesus. Over and over he heard the Holy Spirit whisper, 'Africa shall be saved, Africa shall be saved'. He dedicated his whole life to reaching all of Africa with the gospel, and so it was that 'Christ for all Nations' came into being.

The vision of taking the saving message of Christ 'from Cape to Cairo' still consumes Reinhard. He freely confesses, 'I eat, sleep and drink the vision'.

CfaN attracted world-wide attention in 1984 when they dedicated a tent which would seat over 30,000. It was the largest mobile structure in the world, but such was the pace of progress that by 1986 that was too small. In the Blantyre, Malawi, crusade of 1986, crowds of over 150,000 came to hear Reinhard Bonnke's forthright preaching and to see the mighty miracles of healing and deliverance which invariably followed. It then became clear that the day of the Big Tent was over as far as CfaN was concerned, and with typical generosity, they gave it to another ministry for work in Mozambique.

CfaN's ministry is now divided into two teams, one working in East Africa, and one in West Africa. They currently hold an average of fifteen crusades annually, and believe that the number will increase. Africa is responding as never before. In Ouagadougou, Burkina Faso, in March 1990, crowd attendance at the crusade was well over 200,000 in a single meeting—half the population of the city! Response to the gospel message has been equally exciting in East Africa. Whole nations are being shaken.

CfaN is committed to serving together with other members of the Body of Christ world-wide to bring in the harvest and motivate men and women to Holy-Spirit evangelism.